WESTERNS

Richard Dankleff

OREGON STATE UNIVERSITY PRESS
Corvallis

Library of Congress Cataloging in Publication Data

Dankleff, Richard.
  Westerns.

   1. West (U.S.)—Poetry. I. Title.
PS3554.A569W4 1984   F811'.54   83-21979
ISBN 0-87071-340-X

The paper in this book meets the guidelines for permanence and durability of
the Committee on Production Guidelines for Book Longevity of the Council on
Library Resources.

Acknowledgments

The author thanks the editors of the following publications in which these
poems first appeared.

American Scholar: "Flute Song," "Livery Stable," "The Horse," "The Trail"
Arvon Foundation—1980 Anthology: "Grasshopper Summer"
Carolina Quarterly: "Blizzard"
College English: "Last Winter," "Bud's Daddy," "Flight," "As for Scalp Shirts"
Hiram Poetry Review: "Winter Quarters"
Kansas Quarterly: "Lt. Montgomery Pike Harrison," "Grandfather," "Mamanti,"
    "Mamanti Sings," "Against Big Bow," "Kiowa Dutch," "Thomas," "Kicking Bird"
New Republic: "On a Blazed Tree by the Trail," "Mountain Camp"
Poetry Northwest: "Ben Hodges, Colored"
Prairie Schooner: "The Dealer"
Prism: "Route 56", "Adah"
Sewanee Review: "A Winter's Tale"

Cover photograph used by permission of Boot Hill Museum, Dodge City, Kansas

Special thanks are due the Oregon Arts Commission for a grant in 1978 and the Oregon
State University Foundation for past and present support.

for all the Dankleffs

All lives that has lived;
So much is certain.
W. B. Yeats

Contents

Flute Song

'Twas a curious fact that when Judge Russell played
his flute at night, his horses came and stood
on the cabin porch. When the music soared they paid
such careful heed they seemed to gauge the mood
and quality of tone. Clear nights, wet nights they stayed
and stamped a few times when an extra good
sustained diminuendo that would fade
and seem forever lost (the flute might brood,
as if the Judge were sorry or afraid)
came flowing back crescendo in a flood
of notes as bold as warblers trill when shade
or leaves conceal the singer. Soft or loud,
the Judge's hermit-thrush arpeggios could pervade
so tenderly the Cascade solitude
that daybirds, wakened, may have long delayed
to sleep again (they were so sweetly wooed)
and ghosts of ladies may have tried to wade
the deep horse-pasture creek but, baffled, cooed
forlorn cadenzas back across the glade.
Seldom did a nicker or stamp intrude
upon the solo flute. And the nags obeyed
a strict decorum. When nature called, they would
walk off a decent way and stand; they made
even those tail-high interludes
slow and stately, in deference to the serenade.

River Trader's Ledger

She caught him unprepared. It must have been
like this. The Indian camp at last asleep.
His patched trade-tent a quarter mile beyond.
Toward dawn he wakes, when she comes running.
He knows whose squaw she is, how small her waist,
what roving eyes. (Two ledger pages back,
where figures balanced out the beaver, wolf,
gunpowder and watered pints, it's she who was
the "prettyest piece on the verminous missouri."
Her man had killed "beaucoup piegans & bloods.")
Now she has been beaten—he gives her rum
("she knew I watchd her she would do it")
and gets her out of there. In an hour, gray light,
she's back, dressed in quilled deerskin, with food,
come to stay. Husband? No no, she runs away,
no more hitting, she comes to *him*. Two shots
rip his tent. He curses—the husband, himself.
She moans. The ledger says he made her leave,
go home, he never saw her again nor heard,
with "heard" lined out. The entries that follow—
several times a week, ink faded yellow—trace
his wagon east and south. Twice "big flights
of wild pigeons." "Drank." Mandans tell him
her man cut off that woman's nose and ears.
The margin, with trade figures, has "left hand
my small finger, took 1 joint."

Livery Stable

He leaves the harness room where he sews gear,
cooks and sleeps. Along the rows of stalls
he's tended more than twenty years,
he breathes the sharp high-in-the-nostril smell
of horse. The water tank's inside the door.
Beyond, sun bakes the pole corral.
In here it's cool as a church. Secure,
he and the horses like their mornings dull
and slow, as now, all but a stamping Arab mare.
His old chestnut, eyes closed, rubs on the wall.
His mules look cynical. The bay team stirs,
nickers a hymn to curry-combs. The foal,
as usual loose, comes through the box-stall bars
to snuffle his pockets. Softly cursing them all
he turns to the new day's ritual chores,
puts four at a time in the hot corral to roll,
forks dusty hay in the mangers, from the floor
wheelbarrows manure outside to the pile.
Manure fumes, like an incense, reinforce
the drifting dust from the dry swale
and prairie grasses. Wiping his face, he declares
this life suits him so goddamned well
that most nights in his prayers
he just says thank you . . . . Past the mules,
like a graceful acolyte appears
a glorious buckskin gelding.

Procession

The cart, through smudge-barrel smoke, jolts
on the ruts. To make the horse less uneasy
the driver walks in front, one hand
on the bridle strap. He hopes the smoke,
which stings his eyes, will smother
the yellow fever or cholera vapors.
Except for the cart and the horse's hooves
there are no sounds. Almost no breeze.
Through barely drifting smoke, the river docks,
the road ahead, seem empty. He does not let
the horse, between the shafts, look back.
At corner stations, marked with a cross,
he stops to load the bundled dead.
To help the horse, he tries to keep the weight
of bodies balanced. Two mourning relatives
or friends, or souls confused, follow
the cart in silence, so unprepared for death
they come barehead, barefoot. Three
now, counting the figure he sees waver
past smudge barrels, a little farther back.
Those who are living here must know
his destination, the pasture graves. They
could go direct to the place and wait.
Or go sit in the dead priest's church. Mute,
along the river road, these follow his cart.
That drifting one, back by the rooming house,
may try to follow too, a fourth,
though still so far behind,
so mixed with the floating smoke,
it almost seems there's nothing here
(but some disease) to be afraid of.

Adah

That sound like coyotes may be (when the wind
is this direction) old Adah calling her pigs.
She's a strong mistruster of folks. As for the pigs,
although they wallowed in the river mires
they had nothing to do with those olden
devil-ridden swine. In her sodbusting prime
Adah would have ordered off the place
any fool that called her pigs unclean. Some nights
it slips her mind the bank drove off all her stock.
What does get caught in her head is fear—that thieves
are after her boar and sows. She'll start for the river,
calling out the ancient names they honored
all those years, when she sold none of her beasts
except some litters. That cry sounds run-together
but a hunter walking over her way tonight
might make out that red boar's name, *Ab-
salom* . . . or *Ra-chel Le-ah Ra-chel.*

Posse

Their wagon stands
on the high bank.
Beneath their chopped
hole in the ice
the wretch they poked
is out of sight
till the March thaw,
maybe longer.
"Looks like he's not
a swimming man."
"It beats hanging."
The wind falls and
the heart falls.
By now, almost
too dark to see,
too cold to snow.
Jesus, do we
have it coming?

Blizzard

They heard pounding but couldn't open the door
till both the horses moved. They didn't need
more bodies in this one-room sod house
but knew whoever it was out there would freeze.
Might freeze in here, like the seed potatoes and eggs.
Bracing the door in the wind, they hauled
in a stumbling bundle of snow. "Frog!" the two boys
knew him first, "Antoine, did you bring food?"
"The shack blowed down!" Antoine's scoopshovel must be
outside, he guessed. They left it there, for the door
was latched and the horses back by the door.
One boy: "Antoine, we'll stew our hens,
then we stew you!" Meanwhile the four old hens
pecked horse manure, the wet baby cried, and the wind
sifted snow-dust under the eaves. The boys,
back on the bed, compared chilblains. The two men
talked horses. By candlelight the stooped woman
melted snow for tea, baked bad potatoes,
threatened to burn tomorrow the chair and bed,
kicked at chickens. Antoine described white hedges
of lilacs under the blue skies of Provence
and the drifting blossoms whitening the road for miles.

Bud's Daddy

Blind nearly, but he cooked and thought for both.
They'd filed on quarter sections west of mine.
Last winter, the old man got meat hungry,
and Bud, a fair shot, took to missing.
(That blind man's head was packed with recipes—
stews, pies, goulash, good Memphis hash. He'd talk
chops—fry them fast, don't skimp on lard.
He'd tell us how he used to roast fat geese.)
A couple times Bud sneaked so close to quail
that, after he missed, he set a mark in the snow
to test his gun. His daddy could have talked
for days on crimps and primers, shot charges, wads.
Bud tracked rabbits, kept on shooting, got one—
it's hard to miss them all. The old man said
bad wads break patterns, so Bud should
reload the shells. And watch for prairie hens.
By then, besides the scatter gun
Bud slung his rifle. Zero weather.
More hunts. More good old recipes.
The old man said what he most hungered for
was plain roast goose with brown gravy.
Bud missed more quail. The clincher was a doe,
we think the only one to come through here,
bed down in an alder clump behind snowbanks.
Bud crawled against the wind, got close,
aimed. He says he shut out of his head
all thought he might miss that one. And you know
he missed. After that, he didn't really bother.
No, hell, they couldn't starve with pumpkins, beans.
They got through March, nearly. Now old Bud's
here solitaire, his daddy's back in Memphis.

First Wife

Down on her knees to plant spuds,
Sis raised the dew-soaked burlap bag—
hit twice by a prairie rattler. But
she did, tough as a weed,
push through. (She sent for me
to tend their kids.) That spring, down
two more weeks, she blamed
her old canned corn.
                                    With their last,
another daughter, her down again . . .
and him sad, as ever,
as even in love, taking no blame.
(In the grove he said he'd lain alone
before he met the likes of us.)
Sis propped in bed apologizing—
spring again—she couldn't get out
to plant. Face like a shriveled spud.
Right arm, snake arm, going lame.
She wrote our folks in Illinois:
The first half-section is paid.
Awake in the night coughing, she may
(and no one need feel shamed)
have felt along the shelf for the berry wine
put by for children's croup, or special
guests, uncorked carbolic acid.

The Bone Hauler

When the butcher shop in Indiana burned
he came west, hired on as a buffalo skinner.
Then fall forenoons, he tracked the frosted grass
and hobnobbed with crows. Clucking one big horse
to make the final pull, he peeled the shaggies
and got a name for knack, for shucking thirty a day.
He built a wooden house at the edge of town
and fed his kids fat buffalo steaks.
The summer was for laying K.P. track.
October meant his case of skinning knives.
Four years of that.
                    With the herds shot out in Kansas,
with the railroad stuck at the Colorado line,
he traded his house for a farm—in time for the drought
when even bottom pastures cracked.
To make ends meet, he used his grain-box wagon
to haul in loads of whitening bones to town.
One hundred skeletons, one ton, eight dollars.
As the broad-leaf corn plants yellowed back,
his kids ranged out to hunt and stockpile bones.
Their stacks, inspected now and again by crows,
had a board on top with his name.

Grasshopper Summer

She rushed between her pumpkin patch and cellar
brushing a mass of hoppers from each armload
of green pumpkins. In a voice he hardly knew, she called
to the boy to sweep the sides of the house. Slipping
on greasy hoppers, she pushed the cow to the shed
and walked on hoppers back to the house and sat.
The boy followed her in to ask if bugs
would burn, but got no answer. Home from the field,
his dad, cursing low, brought in clothes
left out on the line and made two trips for harness.
He vetoed fire, "Too many to burn." She sat.
His dad waited; then said "Corn's gone"; then caught
some hoppers on top the table and pinched their heads.
Inside, they hardly heard the sound,
and did not have to watch, though the clouds were still
drifting in from the west. His dad said, "I'll light
the lamp." She stared at the floor.
"That hum," his dad asked, "is that their wings
or jaws?" She wouldn't speak; next day
the same; and on to fall . . . few words.

Nuttall in Arkansa Territory

The three ahead are traveling light
and slow. The fourth lags far behind,
spends half his time on foot, his horse
cluttered with boxes of pressed flowers.
The three ahead still hope to find
the mules they think some Cherokees
or Osage riffraff stole. The fourth has found,
hid down in a cave of grass, one more
(he yells it): *Ixia celestina!*
The three reluctant guides have studied
Mister Nuthead's celestinas.
Back there on his knees, he beckons.
They've heard his Greek palaver.
They yell: Come on! But off the track,
hoping to strike a trail, they all shortcut
across scrub-oak butt-tangling brakes, finally
obliged to lead their four scratched-up horses.
Single file and steaming, they backtrack
through (can't help but learn it) *Quercus montana,*
according to Nut, who's sure-God cracked. And *Quercus*
sounds like *alba.* Half stop—for an acre of nettles
that he says could be cooked. Come on!
The Fort Smith destination forty-fifty miles
by crow. Mules gone to hell or Texas.
Full stop—dismount—Red River buttercups,
folks should admire their strong sepals.
The low sun blossoms reddish roan. The three
ahead are traveling light and slow.

The Dealer

The hour before sunrise,
across the clearing
where two prize horses graze,
a third shape, blurred, drifts darker
than what is left of night. Two halters
looped, two hobbles cut.
Sunrise, across the empty clearing
a south wind dries the grass.

The coin the young man spies
behind the daughter's ear, again
is gold. His three new horses
tied in the peeled-log shed
are eating stage-line oats. The jumpy
station keeper grumbles about
surprise arrivals, law men, alibis,
a stage due here at noon.

In worn sodbuster shoes, work shirt a size
too big, he sits with one small beer.
Drifts down the bar and buys
one sack tobacco. Rolls,
inspects, re-rolls his cigarette.
Though shy, swaps talk on farm
supplies—this town's mule races—crops—
the mayor's famous mares.

So slow the stable flies
are not disturbed, a late arriver
tries the door and waits, is
listening, is counting down four
stalls, unties the bay
that by next month may be
(mane roached, tail short) the fastest horse
in New Mex Territory.

Headed southwest (beyond each rise
the same sun-baked horizon), changing mounts
from five on his lead rope,
aching since yesterday to sleep,
dogged now by three riders
trail-wise as Kiowas
who know the waterholes,
holding on.

On a Blazed Tree by the Trail

The Zion is the LORD.

     Gold sot

—Two white Pigs run off.
  From Walt Jameson.

J. Burks, Capt.—with 18
waggons to Santa Fe—
May 3, 1850. Kioways near
trail—Scalp on pole Wolf
Creek—use scouts

Minny An Drewe 12 Drownd
Cimarron R   1850 June
Rains good grass

August 1, 1850
Pittsburgh Company
Robt Roper stabbed to death
by Jess Strayhorn w/o
justification in quarrel.
Aug. 2 J. Strayhorn tried
& shot. Buried them here.

         tell Ralph Butler
         Calif. wife dyed
         august 17 1850
         Colera. God

—Jon Shot wild hog—Bacon
& blubery cakes—alright—

Lt. Montgomery Pike Harrison

Because he rode a beautiful sorrel
over the ridge alone,
his blue uniform shining and
his brown hair long on his neck,
some Kiowas shot the Lieutenant,
scalped and stripped him, carried off
even his boots and socks.

Because his dead grandfathers
were General Zeb Montgomery Pike and
the General Harrison who was,
for a month, President,
the lieutenant's judicious c.o.
had the bare corpse
thickly coated with tar and
packed between layers of charcoal
in a sealed wagon-box coffin
that the soldiers escorted—"without
inconvenience"—northeast
42 days over plains thick with
mesquite, through a Texas norther
that killed 33 of their mules, across
branches, forks and tributaries
of the Brazos, the Trinity and the Red
to Fort Smith, Arkansas
to be buried with military honors.

Grandfather

"The golden age of the Kiowas had been
short-lived, ninety or a hundred years, say,
from about 1740. The culture would persist
for a while in decline, until about 1875."
—Momaday, *The Way to Rainy Mountain*

Singlehanded killed four Pawnee scouts
    who tried to steal Tai-me, the Sun Dance doll.
Stampeded south the longhorn herds—away
    from the sun's bright buffaloes.
Ambushed sodbusters nailing up barbed wire
    and left them hung on their fences.
My grandfather sits now in the sun.

Rode with Comanches, Cheyennes,
    to strike the Bluecoats, run off cavalry horses.
Fought beside Satank, Big Tree, Lone Wolf,
    each sworn to fight to the death
    (white hunters pushing harder every year,
    more wagons coming, wagons always coming,
    and finally not one buffalo for the Sun Dance).
My grandfather studies his hands on his big stomach.

Watched Lone Wolf, grief-mad, shoot his own horses,
    the soldiers burn every tipi at Palo Duro,
    his daughter, turned Baptist, go off with a Kansas trader,
    his pony herd dwindle to three, and now one, lame.
Having seen many things
    my grandfather talks to Tai-me: Try to remember.
                    Before I die say my name.

Mamanti

When he talks with the owl,
the owl sits on his hand.
Mamanti listens. Then he
talks some more to the owl,
that sits and watches.
And after a while
they have the same head.
He knows what the bird knows.
And when they walk around at night,
he sees what the bird sees.
(Who comes this way raiding.
What dragged Two Deer's baby
back under a ledge on the Salt Fork.)
It's more than just Mamanti's owl
that circles there in the sky.
But then he pounds on a drum and,
after we give some presents,
he tells what he found out.

Mamanti Sings

Your medicine shield
with the red crane
burns on my fire.
The medicine shield
that held your name
twists in my fire.

You turn to smoke,
where Kiowas go
you have no name.
You turn to air,
tonight the bats
brush what you are.

Mamanti sees
you with no name
caught in the wind.
Mamanti sees
the man with no name,
far off, drift south.

Outside the camp
a woman crouches
like a quail.
There in the dark
the woman calls
like a small quail.

Wife left behind,
quit your search,
come back to camp.
Wife left alone,
Mamanti watches
you come here.

The Horse

So alert—they claimed—that no man
would ever see him standing.
(Big Bow knew one man had.)
The old talkers' Great White Steed
roamed the Llano Estacado
like a ghost horse—and alone,
too proud, they said, to herd
with mustangs. (Big Bow counted
in the white stud's own manada
twenty mustang mares.)

Their Great Steed couldn't be hurt—
the old men claimed—by arrows
or even hunters' bullets.
(But in the beginning Big Bow
had found him gunshot in the hoof.
Big Bow cut out the slug,
then healed the wound with moss.
The big horse was his secret.
Killing time between raids,
he'd track down his horse and ride.)

A natural pacer, steady,
and swift as a bird—they claimed,
correctly. Clucked to, he paced faster
than the little mustangs galloped, and gracefully,
with Big Bow proud on his back.
But when they said the Great White Steed
would never break his pace—
that maybe he *couldn't* gallop—
the old fools did not know
what Big Bow knew
with his hands hooked
in the thick mane, his eyes
squinting to slits
(O that white eagle flew),
black hair swept
straight back,
jaws clenched on
a whoop!

Against Big Bow

In the roaring black cloud—far over
our heads—buffalo and whole trees
went tumbling along in the dirt and uproar.
But stupid people say there are no demons,
Big Bow laughs at the spirits.

Good Kiowas heed the Owl Prophet.
But when he told how he died,
how he met his friends in the dead men's town
and brought back dead men's medicine,
Big Bow stood there and hooted.

The Prophet sees the end before a raid begins.
He saw Ute ponies; we drove off their herd.
He saw my brother with arrows in his chest;
my brother stayed home and lived. But Big Bow's
stick crippled the Prophet's Owl.

Big Bow says Kiowas need no prophets.
Big Bow goes off alone and comes home with horses,
with Navaho scalps, with stories of Mexico.
He says medicine men are for cowards.
He unsettles our women.

When demons bring back the roaring clouds,
we pray hard they won't blow away
our tipis and blankets, the rifles, horses—
just to punish Big Bow. For that man,
one stab of lightning!

Kiowa Dutch

Also known as Big Blond.
Born somewhere in Germany. Caught,
young, by Kiowa raiders
somewhere in east Texas.
Could see the dark hatch-hole
of a pitching ship; another storm, the wagons
wrecked; on Bull Hump's horse
that woman's hair. Grew up watchful,
liking raw liver but knowing—
fragments of German, Kiowa and Comanche—
the cracked, windswept world could
split. For his vision
glimpsed invaders and Indians,
frightened men and their women
blown flimsy as sparrows
over the windy plains. He made no name
as a fighter. Caught his eagle—
broke its neck, took no feathers.
Did not run away.
Saw nowhere to run.

Thomas

Treaty talks at the Caddo station bring
a savage chief to Thomas Battey's school.
Huge and unchristened, buffalo-robed,
he sits for more than an hour. Thomas explains
arithmetic to the Caddo pupils.
Then the teacher, beckoned near,
is told by the interpreter:
"Chief say he see your heart.
You love Indians. He love you."

•

At noon recess, a quarter mile
from the school, in the leaves he kicks up
a human skull, which rolls. In the noon sun
it seems to grin. He scoops it
a grave before the children come.

•

"Third Month, 30th, '72. Waking
I thought a voice had asked aloud:
What if thy Lord tell thee to leave the Caddoes
and sojourn in the Kiowa land?
My whole devotion may be required.
But brutal Kiowas—I will resist.
Although a sense that I am not
where I should be continues with me,
I resist."

•

After sick leave at home, Thomas returns
on horseback south. Driven indoors
by the cold to a one-room inn, whose bluff
proprietor retails steer-herders
whiskey from a barrel, Thomas
wrapped in a thin blanket tries
to sleep, tries to disregard
the blaspheming Indian-cursing sons of
Texans with whom he shares the stove.
He journeys to the Kiowas.

•

Kicking Bird says when a Kiowa dies
his spirit travels west, a long way,
to a wide lake. On the opposite shore
dead friends are hunting buffalo
on beautiful swift horses. Waist-high grass
keeps the animals fat. No one is ever sick,
no one breaks bones. White people
were made by the Great White Man, not
the Great Kiowa. Kicking Bird
touches the teacher's hand, but cannot tell
what happens when white people die.

•

Thomas alone in the school tent.
The Kiowa children kept at home,
several with bad coughs. Winter
hangs on. Caddoes have warned the Kiowa chiefs
this teacher makes children sick
by blowing on them. Thomas has blamed
wet feet, wet blankets. But the Kiowas
watch him and scowl. He has explained
superstitions. But the children cough.
This morning, alone in the cold tent,
he buries in his journal "I am sick. O
Paul, the good that I would I do not—"

•

"Third Month, '73. In Wichita Mountains
with Kicking Bird. He too admired
those hues the granite takes—the green,
yellow, rose. We looked with care
at the granite boulders, rough-rounded once
by glaciers grinding. The great rocks
rounded now, a little more each year,
by the unobtrusive lichens.
Gray, tough rock-tamers."

•

The Kiowas' noisy medicine dances
go on for days. Comanches arriving,
drums, chanting, in the medicine house
men with scalps and idols. Thomas,
distressed by their heathenish rites,
prays to his God to light this darkness.
Next day their green-brush roof wilts

28

and the great heat slows the sweating dancers.
To-haint makes medicine for clouds. Groaning,
he scowls into the sun till the sun goes out.
Behind his clouds, the thunder comes.
In the early dark, a storm with rain,
two women struck by lightning.

•

A guest waiting for breakfast, Thomas sees,
beneath a blanket on the lodge pole,
scalps. Neatly dried on bent-stick hoops,
perhaps years old. Instead of explaining school
he draws cats, grinning round cats,
for the host's daughter, about six
and clearly Mexican. His head aches.
Then plums, good boiled pumpkins.

•

He must avoid the lodge of Bear That Pushes.
There, two weeks ago, answering
a call outside, Thomas rose, ignorantly
stepped over his friend's grandson,
as the mother cried out and the others moaned.
Now, in the hour at dawn, four lodges away
he hears the mother wailing.

•

"Eleventh, 18th, '73. Remained
in and about camp. A sky of clouds.
My health worsens. I shall not
establish any school for Kiowas. Yet,
midday, watching the children scuffle,
suddenly I was favored with a sense
that Great Goodness overshadows our lives.
I desire to be thankful."

•

Back in Iowa, home to stay, bone weary,
he wakes from a daytime doze, groaning,
in his aching head certain of the Kiowas'
kicking cantankerous spotted ponies.

29

Kicking Bird

"the chained prisoners were being loaded
into wagons . . . . Mamanti the Sky Walker
[said] 'You will not live long, Kicking Bird.
I will see to that.' Two days later . . .
Kicking Bird died mysteriously."
—Brown, *Bury My Heart at Wounded Knee*

Two days after the Kiowas he had chosen
were carried east to the army prison,
Kicking Bird met the dog that talked.

The dog: "You never can forget."

"I remember stubborn friends
squint-eyed from dreams, who followed dreams."

"Mamanti never can forget."

"He should not call me soldiers' whore.
In prison too he will talk lies."

"The Kiowas never can forget."

"When I chose some, I saved the rest.
The ones I saved throw me away."

"The river runs, remembering nothing."

"I am a shield that splits—one part
falls this way, one part that way."

"The stones remain, remembering nothing."

"Like a dog Mamanti hunts . . ."

"The sun burns, the wind blows,
the bones make soil, remembering nothing."

Lost Trapper

"It was then agreed that either his rifle
had bursted and killed him or his horse
had fallen with him over some tremendous
precipice." —Russell, *Journal of a Trapper*

One day I turned northwest. I just kept riding.
That Yellowstone Plateau was paradise. Grass
horse-belly high. Along the streams, cottonwood groves.
Elk, deer, good deep fat on their rumps. Sheep
on the high benches—I saw them frisk in the snow.
It didn't seem a man would come that near
to heaven twice. The band of Snakes we'd met
the day before, up there along Clark's Fork,
stayed in my head. As I rode back, they came
to mind with a scheme. Besides their kids
I'd seen six men and seven women. That's what
I found—an extra squaw, the sleepiest one,
fat as a deer, and I claimed her. They knew
the steep-ridge land. I knew how, for a while,
to scare off wandering trappers, Blackfeet, Blackrobes.
I had a good mare and the Hawken rifle . . . .
As if we'd got directions in a dream
to keep to the high country where no one
was over us. Like the mountain sheep.
That's how we lived.

Variations on a Tale by Parkman

Francis Parkman stepped from the lodge
and a pack of Sioux dogs rushed to attack.
The big snarler that led the charge
(stiff-bristled as a cactus down its neck)

snapped at the visitor's crotch. It lunged,
it wanted blood at least. The young man's kicks,
which kept it back, spurred the brute's rampage.
Sioux women hustled up and—whacking—

drove off dogs at the pack's edge.
But Parkman saw the Indian men chuckling
as he with these squaw helpers waged
dog warfare *infra dig*. Become a joke,

he stumbled and looked (in vain) for a cudgel
and kicked when the enemy lunged. The brute took
a pocket off before the visitor dodged
through the open flap of a tepee. There it balked.

Parkman watched it wait for him to emerge.
At twenty-three book-learned and politic,
he eyed the dog, controlled his rage,
and mulled *lex talionis* and legendary Greeks.

Share the young man's antique revenge.
Count the red handkerchiefs and trinkets
he'll give the squaw who owns it in exchange
for that big dog—boiled. Smell her cooking
two kettles of meat. Hear him urge
the chiefs to eat heartily. Watch the brute lurk
beyond the banquet, close, out of reach.

Lovers' Lines

The wagon train was camped a ways ahead
getting sorted out. The pair who lingered here
beside their supper fire, by his new wagon,
wore one blanket each. They agreed:
to dash (hell take mosquitoes) right now
down past the rim of light to the creek to wash.
Down in the dark—a splash. Side by side
they listened, hushed, and heard their throat blood
pulse an ancient alarm. Then that beat slowed.
Their hobbled horses stomped a reassurance.
(Back home, she said, she saw a black bear
scramble across the pasture into a gulch, but that
was the last one that anyone there knew of.
He guessed he'd never seen a full-grown bear.)
A wild half-moon came out of the brush
and tangled in the mossy trees before it cleared.
Green wood on the coals made a mosquito smudge
that brought both horses hobbling near for the smoke.
When he stepped back from banking the fire,
she took him into her blanket. That seemed natural.
Out in the dark a prairie wolf cried, the notes
almost significant, like syllables
they might themselves call out into the black
or howl to the slab of moon. They might
follow their own musky bodies into the dim wagon
and there, turning together, hear two cry,
or three, from different sides, and later
feel more voices call than they can separate.

Delay at the Ford

Who knows what hit her—just as her wagon
pulls up the other bank, Missus T kicks off
her shoes, skins that heavy dress up
over her head, and scoots back into the river.
The cows I'm herding along stick up their heads
and stop. Two wagons hub deep in the ford
have stopped. The sun is straight overhead
and maybe stopped and Missus T's white bosom
bobs like ducks. She's mother of boys,
young hellers—already one, *both*
undressed and—splash! race to pull her out.
Or watch her kick. The wagonmaster's pinscher
dances along the bank. Those boys are chasing fish!
The guide's two girls, brown butts—already there.
In a petticoat Ab's wife wades in—and that has to be
Ab, she's going to scrub his back. Missus T,
turned west, can see now what she set off. Sunlight
shimmers from bank to bank. My cows,
dazzled, forgetting they're river shy, hump into
a buffalo gallop that takes them halfway over.
The wagonmaster whistles and points us on,
but next the Schaefers and Krafts. And next
Big John-the-Baptist Johnson hollering hallelujah.

Last Winter

"Before, there had been signs—calves born
five-legged, our town dogs disappeared. Then
two farmers dead the same weekend, maybe
same day. Both cabins bolted inside. Out,
in the snow, no human tracks except our own
and the dead man's. No farms but those for several miles
in that white glare of plain.
                              Family of Germans,
afterwards, came here to visit Bahn.
Came with an extra daughter. Saw the graves.
They called him Christian man.
And Johnson? Steady, like Bahn.
Some weeks those two drove in to town together,
Johnson's wagon. Big men, slow-talking
hard workers.
                    One man might shoot himself. So, maybe
Bahn. But there's his friend, three miles across the fields,
with his throat cut. Let's say, if Bahn was first,
he left behind no ghost. None you would see.
Say he did not. Say, while Johnson honed the blade
(the whetrock there on the table, beside one cup)
no apparition fluttered over his roof, no devil
coyote-tracked through the dried weed stalks.
Still, something. No? Those farmers dead
by human cause?
                    Once we got their graves closed,
a bunch from town rode out and burned their cabins."

Winter Quarters

Fort Larned fleas
eat U.S. rump.
But try to squeeze
one, it'll jump

clear. Compared to these,
our bedbug pets
are fairly easy-
going, they mostly sit.

But back to fleas.
They're our livestock,
from neck to knees
we pasture flocks

of grazing fleas. (Tipis
are better and worse
than barracks—they're breezy,
things disperse,

but the grease agrees
with fleas.) For prairie rat
and mouse sorties,
we got us some cats

tough as Pawnees.
Now the jumping specks
are eating these,
our cats are wrecks,

they're like trainees
that wiggle and scratch
and stretch to reach
the latest itch

but by degrees
they're losing ground.
And a man foresees
while here, snowbound,

no remedies.
The Captain says
a cat can freeze
and his hide for days
still jump with fleas.

Buffalo

You might have admired the skillful pair who circled
behind the buffalo bull and chased him
toward the K.P. railroad cars. At the right moment
the Texan and Indian both dropped lariats
around the huge neck. Their clever horses—
having already cut off the buffalo—dodged
each charge or plunge and played him like a fish.
When the bull's head lowered, the horse he rushed swerved,
while the other, backing, tightened the offside lariat.
They teased him up to the tracks, two more men looped
the hind legs, their horses tugged and the bull
lay stretched out on the prairie.
                                  You might have clapped
for the buffalo, legs trussed, dragged along by the head
on a giant block and tackle. He nearly bucked off their hooks.
He raised a cloud of dust too thick to see through.
You could have heard him fighting the ropes
till the gate slammed shut on their reinforced stock car.
With the dust settled, you could have stepped
close enough to see splits in both blunt horns.
Where the horns curved, the worn-down outside edge.
(The little men on ponies, like waterhole flies,
not even worth your turning around to watch.)
Your breathing keeping time with his huge breathing,
your face near the iron post that bent his head,
your eye caught by that unforgiving eye.

Dixie Lee

1

A boy said I should marry him
and head back to Kentucky.
The time was right for moving on
but eastward is unlucky.
St. Louis, Kansas City, Abilene—
and marriage is unlucky.

Fat railroad man gave me a pass
to the next cowtown. I went.
It's money makes this bughouse spin,
I go where money's spent.
Abilene, Newton, Wichita—
by dawn we have it spent.

Except for the little railroad tracks
only the wind connects.
On some days more than other days
I don't know what comes next.
Wichita, Hays City, Dodge—
I don't care what comes next.

2

I'm a flame that burns for a fiddling man
who cheats and laughs and cheats again.
This time last month I called him mine.
When new girls came, he beat the line,
he took my money up the street.
I never did say love came cheap.

He kindles me when his desire
flares up and up, his fire's my fire.
But his shirt pocket hides a curl
I recognize, his buffalo girl's.
Reason is out, we use none here,
both he and I do what we are.

In the bed we share we're clinker coal.
Smolder and blaze. The story's old.
You know the bed and why I stay.
You know the ancient cry I cry
as I hug the stake. All that can, do.
Where you're looking, flame licks through.

Ben Hodges, Colored

He came from farther south, resources dark,
prepared to deal. His office, Front Street bars.
His hours, night or day. His cards
fanned out in pairs, he hardly had to cheat.
"What takes full house? . . . sure ought not forget,"
he bluffed and beat the odds and raked in pots.
In a town of false fronts, Ben became a master;
competing with slicktalkers he mumbled "Mistuh"
and puffed his bogus claim to an old land grant
till Kansas lawyers, greedy, took a chance
and got themselves dealt in. He conned a sugar-spit
chamber-of-commerce banker to underwrite
a Texas cattle swindle. He paid cash
(part counterfeit) for strays to a pair who dashed
through Dodge ahead of a posse. He always found a way
to have free passes for the Santa Fe.
Folks laughed about the buggers he humbugged,
snipe hunters Ben had left to hold the bag.
But chaff about his money, hints his mug
looked like a rustler's, weren't entirely jokes.
His bid to be Inspector of Livestock
triggered some protests and an unfulfilled
prediction Ben would soon be on Boot Hill.
Which brings to mind that, later, they did give
a proper plot to Ben and dug his grave
beside dead ranchers, merchants, and church folks
"so those can keep an eye on that black fox."

The Legend

"I'll take Clay Allison when
the time comes."

This was the way he strode to meet Ben Thompson
(who lost his nerve, called "Wyatt, what you want?")
and took Ben's guns, conducted him to the judge,
cleaned up bad Ellsworth. This was the way he stopped
the Clements gang coming over the bridge,
sent them like sheep on back to their camp,
and tamed Wichita. This was the way he advanced
through the dust to arrest Sergeant King, jerked
King's guns from his hands, slapped his face,
marched him to jail. This was the way
the big badge shone as he walked straight ahead,
knowing that they knew Wyatt would not draw unless—

At the doors Dodge City merchants, sharpers, whores
and Texas herders watch. He shows them again,
each step closing the gap, steady, ready—
This is the way he strides to meet Clay Allison
killer of sheriffs, Clay here from Pueblo for glory
and one thousand dollars, Clay, now
spurring his horse and screeching and
charging down Front Street to blast and ride over
the white-shirted marshal who walks to meet him,
the incredible marshal who keeps on coming as Clay
slides his horse to a stop,
                              wheels, spurs west from Dodge.

Prairie Dog Dave

recalled with the fourth drink his jitters when
(horseback with Bat a day's ride south of Dodge
in search of missing mules) they topped a ridge
and bingo! faced a party of Cheyennes
with the mules. While things hung in suspense
the two spurred off, outrunning a barrage
of whoops and arrows. Then Dave: "I wouldn't budge
for a few, but we got dozens!" Bat shouted: "Look again—
not even twenty." "I'll bet you—*more* than twenty!"
"Drinks?" "Brandy." Galloping, they shook hands on the wager.
"How do we tell who won?" "We have to count 'em"
Bat said and wheeled his horse. Those Cheyennes blinked
and Bat was among them—pointing—spooking their mounts—
adding "four, eight, ten—"
                          "They thought what you would think,"
Dave recollected, "a trap! They thought they'd got surrounded.
Damned mules stampeded too, all quick as a wink.
We never did agree who owed for the drinks."

A Story Dave Told

for true went back to when, "in their heyday,
horse-rich Comanches sometimes lost their ponies
to Texans, Pawnees, visiting Shoshones,
Arapahoes and such. But *this* horseplay,"
Dave said, "involved Cheyennes. On a sneaky foray
to the south, old Badger and his cronies
spied some buffalo-chasing Comanches. Postponing
their grab, the Cheyennes hid in the brush. That day
they watched those buffalo horses. That night, away
they went—they rode those horses home. Act Two: unknown
to the thieves, Bull Hump's Comanches track the stolen herd.
When Bull Hump steals them back, the Cheyennes are shocked.
But Badger's gang (bear hunting) have no word
of Bull Hump's raid as they—
                          Act Three—toward dawn, knock
the horse herd loose at a camp they find unguarded.
Next, come daylight, Badger's Cheyennes gawk—
they're driving north their own Comanche stock!"

A Toast to Prohibition

led on to temperance jokes—reminding Dave
of the doc who hired our hall for a teetotal talk.
The drys came to applaud, the wets to mock,
and on the stage to see they all behaved
sat Dodge's marshal, Bat, frowning gravely.
Opening strong, the speaker said he would lock
every saloon in Dodge. "Hear, hear." "Take a walk!"
"Skoal!" Bat rose: "I'm here to save
this gent from interrupters." "Whiskey depraves,"
the speaker went on. Snorts. Gun drawn, Bat stalked
to the front of the stage. The speaker: "On the booze
you did not do those things you should have done—"
"Bull—" Bat fired. Shots busted lamps. Folks used
the dark for a cover, Dave
                    too, they left on the run.
Next day the *Globe* reported: "We were not amused."
Those in on Bat's prank called it Kansas fun.
Dave scratched around for a moral, but found none.

False Teeth

set off Dave's yarn: "Big Hat's Crow in-laws smoked
black powder with his Cheyenne kinnikinnick.
They didn't tell Big Hat the powder in their mix
was scrapings from tobacco pipes. His kinfolks'
blend was prime. Back home, he got his poke
of kinnikinnick, spread black *gun*powder thick,
and mixed. He told his squaw, who'd been homesick,
she should puff this Crow pipe. 'Not me. No jokes.'
He tamped. She watched. 'You burn tipi!' she spoke
scrambling backwards as Big Hat picked
a coal from the fire. She heard him grumble he'd get
a Cheyenne squaw who wouldn't sulk
outside in the cold like Crow dimwits
when people smoked
                    KER-BOOM! Mouth full
of pipe, Big Hat, outside to spit,
ears ringing, heard his woman scold some fool
too dumb to smoke, some big numskull."

"The Hermit"

—Dave recollected—"got famous the night he fought
the kicking devil with the cloven hoof.
The Hermit lived with spirits, he kept aloof
from human folks. Just read and thought
and had to do with spooks. He'd cut a dugout
in a hill, three walls were bank, the roof
was poles, then hay, then sod. (This hand's foolproof.
Hearts trump.) Anyway, the night of the famous bout
he woke with dirt in his face—jumped up—a whopping clout
floored him. Back up, he grabbed a leg with that damned hoof—
a devil's? *the* Devil's?—he didn't know which
but knew to hold on tight in either case.
The hairy thing tried to kick loose. The Hermit got pitched
from wall to wall—till he caught
                          the roof, caved in. Face
to face with a bull, he yelled 'Satan, tricky son-of-a-bitch,
this time I kill you!'" "Dave, whoa! That's my ace."
"My heart, son. Yessir, those two wrecked that place."

Last Buffalo in Grant County

Down this ravine—snow drifting—
the gaunt bull under a ledge.
Deep in his head perhaps reverberations
of butting herds, their far-off rumble,
the bellow of bulls in the spring.

Shaggy as some great moss-grown stump—
head turned to meet the wind.
As if he snuffs these Kansas flurries
for quick gusts from the Gulf
and waits for sun.

A boulder—a slowly whitening mound—
humped up in his long patience.
As though the Buffalo Woman
could rise with the coming sun to lead
new buffalo (somewhere her cows are running
and red calves buck at the breezes)
new buffalo out of the ground.

Brick Bond

Their wallows now are corn. But nights,
dreaming of buffalo, he sinks back
to the year he killed three thousand head
between September and Christmas. He hires
the same three skinners to pull hides. Tonight
his driftwood bonfires light the river ford.
Breathing hard, he pulls in deep the stink
of old-time buffalo and goes on shooting.
Here between bonfires, where they
come down to drink: head low,
a huge albino bellows, it's the beast
that people heard Dave Morrow killed.
Brick's old Sharps Fifty roars.
The white tail brushes flies. Three more
lung shots. At each hit, the white hide
twitches and the tail swings. Dream axe in hand,
Brick stands on the drugstore roof—Front Street
is flames—far as that dry torch lights,
the dark herds like slow cloud shadows
drift across the plain. He runs to chop
them down and finds he's home. By his front door
he stands, and tries to think, and slips
into a deepening dream where buffalo
are drifting along the fences like tumbleweeds.

The Bugler

I - 1866

With a Kiowa map, ten soldiers from Fort Dodge
rode south in the Wichitas to ransom captives.
Just at sunset—of a sudden the Kiowa camp.
The sergeant later called it the sight
of his life: there half a mile away
Chief Satanta's people camped by a lake.
On the plain beyond the sunlit lodges, squads
of warriors horseback practiced their maneuvers.
But a bugle call from the camp
ordered the Indian riders into ranks.
The bugle sounded a charge. The warriors
rode in a line, topspeed, to meet the strangers.
With a hundred yards to go—the soldiers' carbines
half-raised—the bugle sounded again and
the Kiowas, making two graceful arcs,
swept to right and left, half on each flank,
to escort the soldiers into camp. The bugler
kept his distance. An Indian said he was nigger.

II - 1874

Dodge City merchants backed the hide hunters
who followed buffalo south to Indian land.
When the men from Dodge put up sod stores
they named Adobe Walls, several hundred
Comanches, Kiowas and their allies attacked.
Caught, the intruders dug in deeper.
They heard a bugler blow a rally, then a charge
that sent lines of painted warriors horseback
against the white men's walls. The hunters
cursed the unseen bugler—when they drove off
the attackers, again that bugle sounded a rally
and called the Indians back for another charge.
Late afternoon on the first day of siege,
a hunter's Big Sharps caught a figure crouched
behind a smoldering wagon of hides. Next day,
the hunters pulling bodies to a ditch
found by the wagon a dead black with a bugle
whom no one identified. His clothes like theirs.
His face-paint Indian. His settled silence mortal.

Captain Henry

The mind retains these pictures (as one keeps,
stuck in an album in a bureau drawer,
creased photographs of shadowy forebears).
They have a use the mind would figure out.
All night after the battle at the Rosebud
Crooks' men buried their dead; at dawn they dragged
their wounded away on travois. Captain Guy Henry,
Third Cavalry—one eye shot out, the other swollen
blind—lay on a blanket stretched between two poles.
He bumped over the rough ground behind an army mule
that jogged to keep up with the column across ravines
that trenched the line of retreat. No one
reports what spooked the mule—when it shied
the captain was pitched onto rocks below. Revived,
wiped off, asked how he felt, he answered "Bully.
Never felt better in my life. Everybody's
so kind." A man named Nickerson wrote down
the captain's words. Again tonight the mind
is turning this over.

Route 56

They rise as quick as thought.
Along this blacktop trail
stranded hitchhikers glimpse
shadows of buffalo.
From deep-plowed wheatfields float
wraiths of sodbusters. Cross-country bumps
a fluttering wagonload of whores. Arapahoes,

still hiding. West—Sand Creek,
where more than the wind wails,
the Colonel's phantom regiment
slaughter their foredoomed foes
while the Cheyenne women shriek
confusion. South—wired upside down, tormented,
an Abolition spy tells what he knows.

On south—shots, horses gallop,
again the gang breaks jail.
Forms fall, and rise, their old wounds aching.
Along this trail bulldozed
through the ancient brush, the scalped
Kansas landscape leads back. On the hill to make
their stand by the orange billboard, ghosts.

Wolf Hunter's Squaw

When wolf pelts brought five dollars cash
and a buffalo carcass made an easy bait,
wolf hunters planted strychnine.

When a hungry wolf would disregard
the smell of men, sooner or later
it swallowed strychnine.

When magpies, ravens, golden eagles
ate poisoned buffalo or wolf,
they swallowed strychnine.

When Pike got south of Crooked Creek
that windy day, he damned the blowing feathers
but planted strychnine.

When Pike and his new Cheyenne squaw
made camp that night along Big Meadow Creek,
she swallowed strychnine.

As for Scalp Shirts

With a good scalp shirt, made just right,
our old-time fighting man was hard to kill.
That scalp shirt man would lead in a charge
and give ground last. He raced in quick,
horseback, to pick up wounded. He tried
to count another coup in every raid.
We honored scalp shirt men as much as chiefs.
A man might loan his shirt to another Cheyenne
to honor him. But if his friend showed fear
he spoiled the shirt. One thing more:
a scalp shirt man whose wife ran off could not
get angry. He could not grab
some horses from the man who took his wife.
He had to look the other way.
He smoked. He had to stand it.
Tall Wolf, who raided Utes for practice
and (no gun) counted coup on three
Pawnees with long-range rifles,
Tall Wolf had two good wives and no scalp shirt.

When the Stars Fell

That muddled next forenoon
the crabby medicine man
(still cross, pox scars dabbed
scarlet) rode off north fast
to talk with more skywatchers.
The dogs prowled stiff-legged.
Painted to fight, the men
rode their horses single file
round and round the camp.
Women wailed death chants.
As if gone mad, the dogs
began to howl like wolves.
Excited children (grandmother
could remember), forbid
to stray, made up a game
in which red stones
were falling stars
and red-mud-smeared children
were scabby medicine men
watching *ai-yee* the sky
with scowls.

Flight

Along the Platte deserted wagons.
Grandmother took my brother and me—
three horses—three days south of the Trail
to her girlhood Cheyennes. More whites
rode through, more cholera cramps—
her friends ran off, they scattered
in family bands, and we went on
south in the time of horses shedding.
My brother came down
with the cramps. Then we went on.
We passed deserted lodges,
we passed lodges with dead. Far south
Grandmother and I made camp
with Kiowas. Their medicine dance
beneath the cottonwood poles
in the house they built for the sun
stopped—a man fell down
with cramps. We ran, that night
on foot we turned back north.
Cheyennes we met knew father
was dead. A big Cheyenne in war paint
rode his horse through camp
and boasted "I can kill
the thing that kills the people!"
But he slid down.
We went north. Red cherry time.
Black cherry time. In the sand hills
north of the Platte, bright noon,
Grandmother lay down.

Mud Springs

Their horses and mules were behind log rails
of an almost Indian-proof corral.
Their barracks was medium strong. But the troops,
holed up since dawn, surrounded, were trapped.
Outnumbered, stalling, they wouldn't come out.
The Indians, foiled, could only shoot.
Some Sioux did crawl to a closer ditch,
but the raid became a sniping match.
The Cheyennes yelled, they cackled like loons.
The Sioux kept banging away with the guns.
No one saw hits—just the gunsmoke puffs.
So shooting was dull. Some Cheyennes left.
What brought them back like honeybees
to syrup? The army horses' neighs.

A trooper—sudden—had run to crack
the corral, he whooped out all the stock
as the Indians scrambled for their own mounts,
astonished and yelling a few more taunts,
then a hundred prizes running loose
and four hundred Indians to touch coups
with coupsticks, bows or arrows, guns—
whoever touched the horse first won
and who missed horses tried for mules
in a rodeo played with Indian rules
by eager warriors and agile beasts
all running wild, at last released
from the tiresome army, running rings
across the prairie outside Mud Springs.

The Trail

On and on down the dust
west from Fort Laramie,
weary, sweat-smeared, we and our beasts
persist. Passing the early starters'
discarded flour tools clothes,
bloated horse carcasses,
sparse grass, grass eaten down,
no one stops. My sister,
six months great, pretends
when our ox teams do finally
founder, she'll start to walk.
I walk (I don't say so) to cradle
my ache. Last week my three-year-old
all one hot afternoon and evening,
peevish, cried. That night
quiet, his rib bones like
a rack, he died toward morning.
More sick now, they all fear
their sieges and vomiting
may become cholera cramps,
attempts to cure that ailment
failing. Ahead, the peaks appear
farther away. Yesterday
past our noon-resting beasts, themselves
eastbound with mail, whirled four
wild Mormons horseback flying
by in dust like fog—with their
spare horses running steadily
ahead—and would not stop,
whipped past us fast and vanished.
When angels take our sons we make
more sons. So say the comforters
to wombs like me. Make bones,
more bones, you cannot make too many.
His candy hid so well
melts. Add to my ache, reckoning
back, that small farmboy with eggs
who urged us buy. Kansas.
Camp time. Down deep-mud wagon ruts
he trudged to us. The banjo-man
began to eat them shell
and all, raw eggs, crunching
crushed shells as dogs do bones
one after one.

Reading Carvalho's *Incidents of Travel*

They hunch dark in the snow. He wants
to say "two birds," but knows he sees
(past where the Utahs' horse herd pushes
close together) two captive Snakes
chased off from the Utahs' camp to starve.
Lines intersect; the distance aids
perspective. Three or four years old,
these are two maws the Utahs can not fill
the rest of this bad winter. The traveler
watches the clouds lour. Snow turns to sleet.
The two Snake children, bent on food, scratch
beneath the crust for grass or roots.

Though a Mormon buys the children
that same day—same page—they infiltrate
the traveler's head, which aches.
The mind retreats, it threshes straw
to thatch a house of words: Snakes at war
with Utahs, captors everywhere
savage, children everywhere
expendable as birds . . . . The mind
can hear an ancient traveler cry:
Who says the sparrows have no horns
that poke holes in my roof?

According to Preuss
(with Fremont, 1842)

Sometimes a buzzard breaks up the monotony.
The prairie . . . flat. Our dried meat's hard as wood.
At noon F brags "I knocked one down,
I got another buff!" (O you little lieutenant,
you don't fool me. Bring in at least the tongue!)
His French-Canadian lumpenpack lap up
his brags. I don't say much. If I were chief—
My latitudes and longitudes, that's what
we came out here to make, exact map-data
observations. Half the time that blunderhead
is out collecting plants; tonight's meal waits
till he comes back with specimens. What good
are they? What good's the boy himself? Kid Karson,
two-thirds humbug, can at least shoot straight.

•

The final straw! F takes me this side trip
to map mole hills—then rain—mosquitoes
mean as devils. Now this: our dirty cook
forgot to pack the salt! Why make fresh meat?—
we have no salt! (Underneath the cart,
mosquito stuck, I smoke my pipe and write
another page.) F says we'll raft the Platte.
What nincompooperheit! But these French fellows
know it all. —Back up the Platte, I found
a spring that looked like sweet cold water: fine,
just what we lacked. I burned my mouth!
That spring's too hot to put the hand and count
past three. I didn't warn the next, Benoit,
I let him burn his mouth a little too.

•

His whims make law. This morning he's all rush—
he hit my horse's tail that stopped to poop.
I don't say anything. These poodle pups
would teach an old dog how to suck an egg.
Last month northwest of Laramie, on top
his "highest" peak, I read myself thermometers,

our patched barometer. F claims
it's thirteen thousand five. I see it's tall.
Maybe thirteen. —But I have hiked die Schweiz,
I know the road beyond Liestal, the daybreak peaks
blooming in alpenglow. The eyes can't hold
that much glory: those glaciers, great ice lakes
in the radiant sun, Mount Blanc to the white Tyrol,
all that snow-crested range. Who threw the knapsack high?
Who jumped like a Yankee Doodle? Who ran as if
the Alps would run away? Ja, that was me.
Tonight the stew is worse. Dirty cooking.

Squaw Man

With ice on the mountain creeks,
he learns to say in Ute
that men hole up like beaver.
He tells her no man's free;
some aren't just tied, they're trapped.
She shrugs. Anyhow, he tries
to say, now she swells with papoose
he's trapped bad. Not drowned
though, one sun-up he'll twist
loose, leave her his leg.

Lice in the robes. Again
he feels one crawl his back.
But the woman turns in his arms
closer. Outside, ice.
He learns to say he's happy he's not
curled up alone. She calls
to the shape that stalks tonight, himself
become a great bull elk. He wades out
toward her, feels the lake floor slope
and the dark water rise.

Mountain Camp

He sits back straight against a pine
and waits for day. To the left, curled cold,
guns by their side his partners nap.
A few coals shine where—two days chased—
they risked a fire. Right, he sees
the three tired horses, tied,
two down on the snow, his black mare up
restless. He plans tomorrow: ride
northeast, locate a hiding place. Between
the coals and mare, he thinks he sees
a shape like a weasel slide by the pile of rocks.
Now is the coldest time. In the dark,
slow paced, this pine tree's creak supplies
the bass for a song he once could strum.
The mare has lain back down.
Tears would freeze. So near
they seem in bullet range, the stars,
whose silence seeping into his head
he chords on the rifle across his knees.

Pages from De Smet

1

She had gleamed, and faded. The Flatheads
gathered, in the dusk, at our log church. They stood
in the snow till the chiefs came out. Inside
the child testified: an hour before, just as
he entered his hut to try to learn the prayers,
to him, Paul, appeared Our Holy Mother.
As if she rose from the cloud of his breath:
her feet were bare and did not touch the floor,
her garment foreign, of white cloth.
Her heart or bosom beamed like our Yule star.

A Flathead orphan, this five-year-old is reared
by an aged and good woman. All we hear of both
helps us rule out guile. Today the chiefs—
excited still—have questioned the child.
His shy answers add details that clarify
and seem to fit: her heartbeam lit the hut—
his fear left—she smiled, spoke Flathead,
told him her name. She was pleased that his
new name is Paul and the mission is St. Mary's.

How shall a priest improve their faith?
They humble us. They trust we bring them truth
and never seem to think that we might err.
Paul comes to tell me: when the Mother gleamed
and he still trembled, the words he had not learned
were there, like his name. I hear him recite,
he has the prayers perfect, never stumbles.
His eyes are open still upon some glory.
She may have come to him once more, in a dream,
as he believes. Inquiries will continue.

2

Far off on the hill we see a Blackfoot scout
stand on his horse and hold his gunstock high
to signal *buffalo*. The hungry families rush
to break camp, collect their stragglers, pack
the gear on horses the boys have already caught.
The hunters rig their fastest buffalo horses.
And those who galloped ahead come back. They all
dismount to invoke Our Lady (killing Crows
or meat, they think her medicine always works).
Now three Ave Marias. For extra luck
the hunters give the prayer again in Flathead.

Pursuing the herd, the men race out of sight.
I watch the Blackfoot women's brutal knack
dispatch the downed cows and a bull. They hatchet
and slice warm flesh. Children I baptized chase
across the plain—and catch—pull down
an arrow-punctured calf. They stab its neck
and dabble their fingers in the throat blood
and lick them. We think His world was different once.
Butchered out, stacked on new hides: slabs of rib
and shoulder, livers, tongues, piles of fat.

By dark, on the sticks around each fire, chunks
of fresh meat cook. And farther out, the dogs
so offal-sated they choke back up their gobble
to chew again. Such—O Lord—bloodsoaked abundance.
We kneel with wondering thanks. Around the fire
for their Blackrobe, the women have stuck
thick slabs of hump, each with a wreath
of tongue or greasy kidney. And my mouth waters,
my stomach growls. To all who must partake
I offer grace. We share like brothers.

3

These Mandan parents boast I baptized them
twenty years ago, when their own parents
with Rees and 'Ventres who survived smallpox,
made this village. (I breathe their pox dead yet,
but treasure the souls who would not die unblessed.
Till I arrived with sacramental water, those dared
endure. May they, in heaven, intercede for me.)
This trip I'm sent to talk peace with the Sioux,
whose messengers are late. I give the day
to Chief Soaring War Eagle—he wants
the Mandan babes baptized.

Seated, in their earth hall, over two hundred men:
a Mandan speaker lauds the priest who comes
from both President Lincoln and Chief Blackrobe.
Then Soaring War Eagle speaks of many things.
At last the mothers are brought inside. By pushing,
space is made to get them all in a triple circle
with their two hundred and four small children.
I stoop or kneel, anoint them one by one,
repeat the names, and give each child a medal
from which the Virgin smiles.

All is well—till I reach the second ring.
In a moment we have an earsplitting din,
for a babe takes fright of me with such piercing
shrieks that a dozen erupt in tears. When this
uproar subsides to sobs, another child (Am I
a bear?) screams in terror. His howls set off
a score—and they, more! The dogs outside
burst bristling into our pandemonium
but, yelping, get flung out. Soaring War Eagle
curses in Mandan and Ree. I proceed.
Our Lady is honored today with a shrill chorale.

Drumhead Court

Tobacco balled in his cheek, this fellow may
be lynched for the sullen face. Never mind
just how he got the team of mules. Our own
Lieutenant Wag, the judge, demands "ORDER!
Bona mors. Counsel for defense
has pled with highfalutin eloquence, *et cetera.*
But qualities of mercy shall not further strain
the patience of this court. *Et cetera.* Let Hank
take three steps forward. *Dulce est
pro patria mori*, Hank." The cat regards
the mouse.
        "Defendant has a lean and thievish look.
Such men are dangerous. *Bona mors."* Pause.
"The evidence: to wit, two mules, brown, U S brand,
is hereby judged conclusive. Sentence is:
Hank shall be hanged from the wagon tongue
those men are hoisting upright by the tents.
Five minutes granted to prepare his soul,
et cetera. Court adjourns." The prisoner sinks
to his knees, beseechingly. Standing guard
as straight as if he'd never kissed an arse,
our corporal with a two-inch rope
knots an enormous hangman's-noose.
A Slovak private greases the loop.
Two minutes. Talk expires. One.
                    Hank
abruptly scuts across the prairie, already
fifty yards ahead of the captain's greyhound,
both man and dog urged on by the troopers' yells.
"If he can hold that speed," the corporal estimates,
"he'll make Fort Laramie by supper time."
A detail rides to whistle back the dog.

Monster

It had a thick tongue
but could snuff and make a sort
of bear bark, part grunt, part
almost a laugh. Not much cause
to laugh. Unless maybe before,
tumbling with cubs in the den and padding
around its valley loose, before our men
dug it out and roped the stub neck
and hump. Looked full grown. Male
for sure. Shag-haired in patches.
Called it Digger, once it was dragged
through several cricks that soaked off
the crust. It even got to looking
like somebody's poor relation,
not that that meant a whole lot.
Would try to cuff those
that tugged on its rope.
Would make horses snort.
Some days watched us and watched us
but could not say what bad luck
brought it where it was.
The young preacher said "God.
Whose judgments are a great deep."
Even he did not touch it.
By the end, scrabbling under our wagons,
it tried to make up to the dogs.
The dogs would not have it, snapped
when it crawled close. Two of us
gave ourselves the order, past Fort Hall,
to lead the creature way up a draw
and cut the rope and ride off fast.

Woman Trouble

The wind had to blow . . . our patient animals
had to follow our directions . . . we trailed west,
by our own choice or maybe not, two or
three miles an hour, and came to a lone wagon.
A man and child waved. My man veered us over
to them and stopped. They'd sat long enough
for the dead oxen, nearby, under a little sand,
to be already swollen. Finally the two men pulled
the wife out of the wagon. She couldn't bear
the thought of what she would have to walk away
and leave. I lifted their tads—both girls, wide-eyed—
on our two steadiest mules to straddle the packs.
My stomach was five months big, that made me clumsy.
She cried most at leaving her walnut chairs—
for a quarter mile she carried two in each hand.
So no one later would break them up for fuel
I helped her hide them, in a little ditch. Toward noon
as we walked behind, she called the whole thing her fault,
said she was the one let the oxen drink bad water.
(But trouble's a drifting seed nobody made, sprouts
in the dark, and grows, swells—maybe there's no way
to hold it back.) I didn't know yet what I
could bear. We walked more to one side, but the sand,
scuffed by the mules, came sifting and sifting along.

Campfire Talk

"Once when the rest were arguing
and arguing religion, Silent Tom
told how his steamboat crew found buffalo
mired in quicksand. Along the Upper Missouri,
about three hundred buff that couldn't move.
They had some sports aboard, fellows who rowed across
to the trapped bulls and even stepped on their backs.
They hunted out and shot the biggest heads.
Tom claimed the steamer waited half a day
while men rowed over to cut a trophy head.

As Tom poked coals—not so smoky as this wet-stick
abomination—the Deacon said 'God witnesses.'
We all let that go by. Tom said the worst
part was—in near the bank—some buffalo
would beller. Coyotes ate at their rear ends.
At the end with eyes were knots of crows.

Tom poked the fire. A boy said 'What's your point?'
'The point,' the Deacon said, 'is Tom is drunk.'
'The point,' Tom said, 'is God don't watch,
born blind or cried his eyes out.'
It sounded like a coughing, then
'Mock God and die'—almost before
the Deacon's snub-nose gun flashed,
Tom folded like a hinge. Well, some
said string the Deacon up, and some were scared,
and he rode off before the burial."

Will Drannan Tells It

1 - Denver City

Rode up to a crowd by Cherry Creek—
man said a hanging brought them there.
That was a trick I never saw. I stopped
to stare. They had a murderer, hands tied,
sick-looker name of Gordon, with a few last words
I didn't hear because he cried.
Crowd stood around. Kid brought Gordon a chair.
Big minister supplied a prayer. We clapped.
More standing around, till the sheriff stirred,
led Gordon to their scaffold, roped
his neck, and sprung the trap. No struggle,
he just twitched. Then who drove up
but my old friend Joe Favor. Followed his buggy
to the Jefferson House, and trout for supper.

2 - Cuckoo

I trailed the fellow's wagon tracks
circling round and tried to figure out
his course. About dark, found him clear back
on his own dried-up ranch, one hind wheel caught
in some brush. Down there on his knees
in front of the mules and slapping at their forelegs,
telling those jacks the Baby Jesus
loved them and loved all critters, begging
his jumpy team to kneel down and pray . . .
loco. Somehow that little Christ
got in the fellow's head to twist his wits.
Person don't know hardly what to say.
That hot day he sure gave his mules a sweat.
Later on we heard he got all right.

3 · Courtship

Said she'd regarded me to be a gent.
Told her that's what I was.
Said well she hoped my knife would bust.
Told her it never bent.
Said she'd pray heaven that I'd repent
my (what she called) blood lust.
Told her no need raise such a fuss
for a little Indian hair. Said what she meant—
But told her shush, told her I'd make the talk:
scalps will be had, because man wants to cut,
and whoso doubts it better learn how to shoot.
Told her to watch out where she walked
because her own chestnut topknot
could end up tassels on my Cheyenne coat.

4 · Business

We'd stay in the Kioway camp a week before
we let them buy, Bridger and me.
Then our big day, quick dealing back and forth,
two buffler robes for a looking glass—or three,
good hides! We had them beat. The bucks
ran all that barter. They made the greasy squaws,
that skinned and stretched and tanned, stand way back
and shut up, they did browbeat their squaws.
(We'd meant to grab ourselves this buffler trade.
No use, we had to work for Robidou and Bent.
We'd bring those buzzards thirty packhorse loads
for a hundred dollars' worth of junk and beads.
So they got richer, back in Bent's stockade,
every trip that me and Bridger made.)

The Revenge

John Chisum once, the story goes,
told hands who didn't agree
to his off-season cut in pay:
"Cowpokes who work for me

do not tell me what wage to give."
"Sweat labor!" "Pack your gear.
The work's caught up. Cook needs a rest.
Try living on hot air."

They packed their gear and said the cook
had made their bellies shrink.
"That pennypincher's like his boss."
"Their mule-meat goulash stank."

They packed, then hunted for the cook.
"Where is Old Chisum's whoore?"
"He wouldn't keep on working here
if he was getting poor."

And then they thought—because the irons
were there in the corral—
to brand the cook. John Chisum's brand
was a long bar called the Rail.

"We'll give him a taste of something warm."
"For the rest of the sucker's life
he'll be marked Chisum property."
"He'll cook for the boss like a wife."

They dragged him from behind a shed
while the cook struggled and kicked
and tried to get away. In the coals
the iron was a red spike.

They held him down beside the fire
and tore off his white coat.
They burned the Rail on his back ribs
and left him curled in the dirt.

The Agency

Our grown boys look for shade.
They have no coups to tell,
almost no dogs to watch. They sit
and wait. Or track down squirming lizards.
They don't even want to carouse.
They sit and squint down the road
that winds along to the Fort,
safe as the milk cows, switching flies.
To go run off some beautiful Crow horses
a man might ride the railroad train,
if he could get the permit,
if he had medicine to fool the Crows.
New kinds of flies pester the face,
our babies wake up cross. Our women hoe
in the dust and plant squash seeds
because Dog Shooter says: Grow squash.
He walks on his porch and squirts tobacco.

Col. Fremont Broods

Deaf to commands, a column in my brain
resumes its march. The trail beside the lake
crooks down to that predestinated beach. We face—
and can't escape each other—a dozen braves
with fish and guns. Mechanical, straight
toward my fifteen they walk, the same as that day,
my men tense, whom I their Captain tight rein
but can not turn, again the same—
as if the Captain dreams and can not wake
to reconstruct events nor change
the cadence set. The Indians watch the trail.
Our two lines must meet. Their guns a rod away,
between the lake and us they file like shades—
not one will raise his eyes toward our invasion
nor turn his head, necks die-hard stiff with rage
or pride. And both lines deaf as fate.

Old Bill

(d. San Juan Mts., March 1849)

He'd heard of better tribes and lived with worse.
These Mountain Utes would do, he'd say,
they made him feel their enemies were his.
And then it all went bad. Spring, '48,
to help Ute friends Bill packed their furs
with his to sell in Taos, where he stumbled
through a rum-dum long-week binge. Flat broke
in a bad dream, he bummed revival drinks,
someway got hired for mountain scout
by the army, fought beside the troops (and drank
alone, glum, as the trancelike summer
blurred), was shot in the arm (Apache sniper),
himself picked off Apaches and accidentally
Utes at Cumbres Pass where the Utes cursed
the friend who now had twice sold out the tribe,
who should have stayed far south of the mountains
but (winter) went back up to guide Fremont's
snowbound fourth expedition and starve with them
(Bill half asleep on his feet, who should have known
the route they took was mad) till Fremont led
the shaky survivors down the slopes to Taos.
The bad dream jumped ahead into March: Old Bill
someway back up in the drifted mountain snow
to salvage the expedition's gear, Mex workers
abruptly gone, his pack mules humped
with dug-up cached equipment, saddles, guns,
medical stores: numb, stumbling toward an end,
he must have watched them coming across the snow
about the way he had foreseen, but slower, some
almost lazily cutting across the drifts, meaner,
the Utes come now to wake him from his dream.

On the Upper Columbia

Elkanah gave Old Chief an ultimatum:
If you keep your infernal dogs, we leave.
After a week of talk, the Spokanes chose
to kill the dogs and keep the missionaries.
A cynic may guess the Indians hankered for
a feast of dog. Or guess Old Chief's committee
thought five to ten starved curs per lodge
less apt to pay than a Christian mission. But
Old Chief said wise men learn to winnow good
from bad.
        The dogs, before their end,
chewed holes in missionary tents. Fiendishly
cunning, they waited till a sleeper sank
through feigned snores to real, then wriggled in
and crawled wherever food was cached.
They dragged off moccasins, a leather halter,
straps. Elkanah woke and found (as ugly
as the Toad in Eden squat at the ear of Eve)
a piggish mutt tugging his saddle-pillow.
Black-gowns and Protestants agreed
the multifarious Devil prowled these camps,
tail hooked low, and snarled hungrily.

Mary Walker

She packs her four new laying hens horseback
from the southern mission post. "They'll croak
before we're home. Too far"—Elkanah, unwell,
spreads his gloom. The trail meanders on (and what
is crooked cannot be made straight). Two nights,
waking, she feels Elkanah shake in his sleep.
Her hens no longer cluck. By the third camp
the prized chickens have shaken down to one
meek survivor, doomed, too fuddled to crawl out
of the bag. An Indian rider brings an envelope:
"Alice Whitman drowned—can you return
to funeral?" Too far. She sobs for the limp
chickens, baby Alice, husband out of tune,
more. Gathering wood, she goes off to bawl
alone, at dusk, for all her vanities. Then back
to the camp (let thy heart rejoice in labor)
to stew the fallen hens. Next day under the sun
they ride on north. At the ford, in the brown mud,
brilliant black-winged Mourning Cloaks
are opening closing quick, as if death winks.

The Carpenters' Women

Then Campbell caught his woman slipping out
to meet an Indian. He thought the child
she had conceived was Indian. Scrubbing clothes
I heard Campbell send her off. (But she
sneaked back and hid. By then husband,
whom I count on, gone to the southern missions.)
At our new house, Campbell worked with Adams
on the chimney wall. And it was Adams' halfbreed
daughter or else her mother who showed Campbell
his woman hid in the cornfield. So Campbell
found her, horsewhipped the pretty shirt—
blood on her arms—big Campbell sobbing too
and he New England born! (Husband,
who never had to cry for me, might
have said what's right, but gone, still.)
I had berries to dry. I made more soap.
She wouldn't let him throw her away. Before sunset
she came back, cut arms and all, teasing at him.
Then his desire was toward her.

But when those two men started to dig our well
Adams' woman made them send Campbell's
straight to Fort Colville. They did. Four days.
(Though husband here again, I don't know what
he knew.) Five days. Down at the well,
Campbell, both his big freckled hands inside
her flower shirt: I saw. His woman is back
to stay. So Adams quit—he said the females
couldn't get along—and took his family away.
On horseback Adams' daughter looked softer,
more grown up than I knew. Her mother thought
she'd marry Campbell! But off they rode
to the Fort. Within the week Adams here again,
so happy, like a runaway boy, rid for good
of his "old woman"—till next night she rode in,
the girl too, and Adams hugged them both tight.
The wind goes south. The wind goes north. And we
turn. I hold husband tight, desire
whom I desire and say we're in God's hands.

A Page Not Sent

Big Shoulders threw his pay food on the ground
when I paid him off. He'd tried our two-man saw
for a day and couldn't keep up.
Even The Thief dreads ridicule—I hear
he's in a rage because I say he steals.
He threatens not to come here any more.
And Spokane Garry's heart resists
Our Lord. Garry knows more English
than I shall ever learn Spokane,
but he goes off for months. He won't speak
for me again on Sundays, because the people
jaw him. They point at him and laugh.
And I, who trail along from camas grounds
to salmon racks (while they gamble,
make heathen medicine, change their wives),
who study late and teach, or try, now six years
(while they're ingrate and unconcerned),
I read again Luke 9: The plowman, hand to plow,
shall not look back, much less turn back.
And Quarterly Reports shall not be other
than hopeful. I cannot go home.
                                    Tonight
they sing like frogs the medicine for rain.

72

The Independent

He came unsanctioned by the Board,
as if the Lord Himself sent this distracted man
and blessed his long hands on the cottonwood planks.
This carpenter who built Wailatpu School,
his work so good that in six months the mission
doubled his wage. This jack of all tools.
This master of beams and kingposts who, toward fall,
became in fact a father and, day by day,
in splintered revelations came to be
Chief of all the Board's foreign missions.
A winter guest heard Whitman's carpenter—
sharp axe skinning timbers—agonize: where next
to send Christ's Love. Some shivering Indians
heard him order the mission shacks burned down.

And what has been will be: wracked
by that foreknowledge, he watches them watch him,
in May, as Hudson's Bay men guide his family east—
the three-week plodding trip along the Snake
horseback, a desert place of crumbling rock,
the Devil's roost. Then Babylonians at Fort Hall.
In 1841 the rendezvous are over but, as he
foresees, a trapper can pack the family on
three hundred miles more to the Green. There they
will stall. No travel farther east. So the long
backtrack—he recognizes rocks—to Fort Hall. Again
the sunbaked trail along the Snake, the escort's
hard shortcuts, the same black firepit holes.
He hears himself rehearse—day after windy day—
a babble of parables. The child cries.
The wife just keeps riding. In September
they reach Wailatpu Mission, where no one
says: Welcome back.

The climax will not take him by surprise.
For Christ's birthday, down in the Valley
the carpenter for love will reenact
the noon of Love. He can not nail
his two arms wide, but practiced craft
will drive exactly center a bridge spike
through the left-hand palm. And he can kneel
in the fireplace coals till his arms crack
and on the third day die.

Precipice

Almost each turn my horse slides rocks.
The trapper, behind, on his tall horse bumps mine
and says: Go faster.
                    What manner of God
can so up-end and crush the earth's
foundations? Here the trail (I hold in
my moan) a scant foot wide crumbles, it is death
to fall, and just ahead a fresh cave-off
more narrow still but: Faster, Missus, or
we all slip. (I must not fright my careful
horse with a sound.) Threatening our heads,
this jut of rocks, coiled scrub-cedar roots
that will not hold—and off below,
far down, the river twists like a worm of doubt
that eats away what was good ground, that will
take even this last ledge
                    —and a whitish bird
floats high as us, a rag just out of reach
to flag surrender, half-turning
(white as His transfigured coat—wondrous
God, teach Thou me), floating
near us, but not with our dead weight,
not with throat to burst, O not
with the beast that snorts Ha, ha,
behind me and lays ears back to bite
my horse that picks its way.
The trapper: Go fast!

Alice

Our youngster's name runs through the lines
her proud grandfolks mailed west around
Cape Horn. Their out-of-date congratulations
rewake, this moldering fall, our grief
for Alice, drowned five months ago.
I recognize my own old phrases—"singing
her Cayuse hymns," "the clown," "bolder
than Indian children." The Cayuse women frowned,
I wrote, to see her toddling at an age
when they keep their babes bound on frames.
By now perhaps, in a ship's dark hold
rounding Cape Horn . . . the grandfolks' crate
that could arrive next fall—with clothes to fit
a four-year-old "babbler of Cayuse English."
Cotton stockings, flannel gowns, a doll
to scold for bouncing the bed, wading the river.
This time next year, my folks will have found out.
Their letters, her end known, will come
year after next, with out-of-date condolence
that won't let lie down to stay—"her mother's
constant companion"—what must at last stay down.

Providence

Long held back in the drifted Sangre de Cristos,
bound for Bent's Fort on the Arkansas River
and floundering all day Saturday in soft snow
waist-deep each time their pack mules (breaking
the crust) must be dug out, Whitman,
his friend, and the guide meet George Bent. "If Doc
could get to the Fort real soon, he'd catch the traders
headed for Saint Louis." They offer Whitman
the strongest mule. With it, packing very light,
he could push through in one more day. That day
the Sabbath. He makes his choice, he knows
he's going east on the Lord's business,
so hurries on alone, comes to the Arkansas and
half-glimpsing the Fort far upstream, turns there.
Tuesday his friend arrives at the Fort: no Doc.
On a guess, the friend starts west, upriver, cuts
the bends in his haste, and next day talks to Indians
who had met such a man lost in the blowing snow.
They sent the man down to Bent's Fort. Shortcutting
back to the Fort, the friend is there Thursday
when Whitman trudges in, chastened by God
for having profaned the Sabbath. He testifies
that he, whose life should be an example, broke
the Fourth Command; for which, divinely bewildered
he rushed upriver through drifting snow or clouds,
along beyond the loops and bends and
hooks of the Arkansas, till Utes or angels
gave him the sign to go back, follow the river down,
and punishment ended. Hungry, happy,
he will (with a nap, a fresh mule) push on,
God willing, and find the Saint Louis traders.

Marcus Whitman

He trekked west in '35 for trial by God.
He knew wisdom began in fear of the Lord
(had still to learn that deeper: when he planned
to leave his mission post, God took his child).
He knew hell burned, for all whose hearts were bad.
"Yet I am rock. Let Him use me to build."

Himself helped build the wagon road,
sawmill, granaries, gristmills, and toiled
to school surly, at last murderous
heathen souls who could not find
the strait gate that led
to Doctor Whitman's heaven. "Cayuse
good hearts. Talk us good word."

God pushed him hard. He strove
to heal, he did the best he could.
His granite millstones ground
their corn and wheat for all,
Indians and immigrants alike.
He fed them also with the finest bread.
"O Lord, search me, and know my heart."

Chopped, shot, left for dead
he lay all afternoon
beside the broad road of destruction.
"Can we stop your blood?" "No."
"Have you peace of mind?" "Yes."
And his heart magnified the Lord.

The Volunteers that came upriver found
the Whitman station burned,
even his last gristmill, except (in the rain
aglint) its two great stones.
A scout, years afterward, recalled
"His mouth was nearer like General Grant's
than anyone else I've knowed."
His time was 1802 to 1847.

Theophilos Degen

Across the page, out of the dust he marches
beside the two-ox team, unable to make the gigglers
on top the cart sit down. Man, oxen, children
wester, caught in a mile-long wagon train.
The oxen were yoked in line four months back,
outside Saint Joe, hitched to a farm rig
that shook apart and made this two-wheeled box
they drag across sage flats. Beneath the cart,
the slap and scratch of broken-top sagebrush. The man
marches. He queries the oxen *"Was ist los?"*
and keeps them moving. Somebody Captain
ordered him down the line a month ago
to set the child's fracture. He remained
to bury the last parent. Grimed with dust
three of his girls, *westlich Lausmädchen*, clamber
both sides of the cart. They trade complaints
with the girl on top whose leg is wrapped in splints,
or practice childbirth pains, or call *"Ach, Doktor!"*
and faint. (He gives the team advice and keeps
them straight.) The gigglers tag the sister who chaws
sage snuff, they chase the moving patch of shade.
Two boys, older, worry along behind with the cow.
For the six he acts as father, connects
their transient route with his, these days, here,
October '44 west of Fort Hall. The book
knows where the children died. The doctor
westers off the page. Part of a shadowy order,
he shares two paragraphs and a dusty footnote.

Melting Time

"Have you heard from heaven? Has the singing
stopped?" —Henry Spalding, *Diary*

Souls flock like doves to God—and two
hardened trappers melt, full of Love
as my Nez Perces, called to Love
by their example. C came to the door
last weekend—stood outside—he felt
a strange distress or guilt, an urgency
to talk. Beneath the stars, remembering
the years he dwelt in wickedness,
he dissolved in tears. I spoke of grace.
He left. He tried but could not sleep.
Last night both mountain men returned
for help—both in heartfelt distress—
we prayed at the kitchen table—their tears,
the living water, streamed. Struck hard,
headstrong still to resist, C knelt,
a desperate case. E struggling wept
for sin with strange women. To God belongs
all credit—He dealt the blows—He joys
to see them in the dust. His angels
thrill when men like these repent
abominations. I know a father
whose sons rode off to waste their wealth
in a far country, with riotous living,
till the famine came. Then those two sons
fed swine, themselves ate swill
and lived in filth. At last they straggled
home, and knelt, repentant: "Father,
we have sinned, we are not worthy." "Nay—
come—for these my boys leave wrong
for right—were lost, who now are found—
were dead, who live." O strong in heart,
He is amongst us though we knew it not,
He tunes the land with tearful song.

News from a Far Country

Good friends: Your pine barrel, transshipped
at Fort Vancouver to a river boat, came tight
and dry, in two years' time. Our thanks inadequate
for the many gifts. (Proverbs 11:25)
Your cotton shirts reward our Indian workers.
So your kind gifts (The Lord hath need of them)
rebuild the mission schoolhouse—80 students in winter,
among them several chiefs. They copy in Nez Perce
our strict translations—first, The Lord's Prayer,
Beatitudes, The Ten Commands. They love to sing
on Sabbath—every day—their favorite hymns.
With hoes and ploughs from us, some of the men
grow wheat. Some will raise cows. And sheep,
when the wolves are killed. Already Mrs. Spalding's
class can spin and weave our little wool.

The station's daily cares interrupt my page.
This noon the house was full of Indians.
The sick we treat with calomel, ipecac, quinine,
jalap. They like bloodletting best, one noon
I had six bleeding—they to stop the blood
themselves when ready. Bowel complaints.
Lung ailments, coughs. But, coming to us,
they put us under obligation to give, and give
again, they favor us by using up our pills—
"we leave the conjure men, we let *you* help."
Somehow, our help puts us in debt to them.

                                    And yet
this field is full of promise. (They that be whole
need not physicians) We trust them with supplies,
the good keep faith. The chaff—

                              I must write
between jobs. Again, our thanks for barrel
with children's shoes, good razor, water pail,
chisel and saw, small shovel, underwear.
Our Indians learn to work. Twice the number needed
help cut wheat, tramp straw to chaff, then winnow.
Others are sawing boards. I pay each evening.
For some, seven or eight loads of ammunition.

For boys—a comb or fish hooks. Women—thimbles,
beads, shirt cloth. This year God put
300 bushels of wheat in the station bin,
besides the grain in stacks. We praise the Lord
of the harvest, that He has blessed the fields.

We heard James Polk is President. —We do stop
twice a day to eat, as now. Your rich donations
remain much in our minds, the compass, map,
good paper——I need ink. Your iron-hooped
pine barrel we sawed midway for two washtubs.
I should remark all property here belongs
to the Mission Board. We have no salary, just
our small allowance—enough for who prepare the way,
root up the thorns and break up the fallow ground.
We hope through love to God and man to see
most of the Nez Perce people brought to Christ.
Until that time, we seem to owe them more
each year—I give out medicine
until it's gone, them some revile me
(Matthew 5:12) and blame me for the sick.
We gave our heifers to those Indians who were
most careful of stock. Then our two best milch cows
were shot. The all-night gamblers burned
our best rail fence. When I reproved gambling,
three nights attempts were made to burn our house.
And though I love this folk, He that will come
will gather His good wheat into the garner
and fire the chaff.

                    Three years from now
Liza will be eleven. Henry nine. Martha three.
If they be spared. I wear a shoe eleven inches,
Mrs. Spalding ten. For Indian trade—shirts,
needles, fish hooks. Direct your barrel
to Henry Spalding, Oregon, c/o the Board
in Boston, freight prepaid.

Temptation of John Townsend

The burial sites had Indians near
till now. This lone canoe, Chinook,
up fourteen feet in a cedar crotch, surprises
the doctor with its otter-robed young squaw.
Neckband: ioqua shells. Face: *aristos*.
From nose to crown of head: almost a straight line.
A mummy, but patrician still, and still
bewildering. There is no morbid odor. Her state
of preservation is worth analysis.

That night, braced in the tree's fork,
he lowers the lady gently with a rope.
His heart beats the wilderness beat.
In the dark he straightens her burial wrap,
her belt of beads, and carries her down the beach
to his canoe; thence, unseen and rapid, back
to the trading station to catalog the data.
Lamp turned low, he pins a rip in her shirt.
The lady, enigmatic, keeps her secrets.
Like Cleopatra smuggled inside a rug,
she rolls into a native mat. He neatly
stitches it, then folds her in a crate
beside a box of study skins. She is
to wait in the station shed, till she
can join him at Fort Vancouver.

The schooner brings, instead, a bill
for three trade blankets. With a note:
"we send 1 box. Indian found tracks
to beach—her brother—got so wild
we had to open things—Dr T will find
his lot one item short. due us £ 9."

A Winter's Tale

Half drunk, the factor said he'd seen,
under his feet, his faithful wife
caught in the lake's clear ice. He thought
he'd chased her off. Correcting that,
he thought he'd dreamed she fled—across
the lake, out far on the glassy film
before it broke. The next hard freeze
turned her to stone.
              If you had gone
with us to find her there suspended and
leaning slightly backward in the ice, she
locked beyond concern for selfish lovers
or the loose braids frozen afloat,
her stare might have held you. As when,
perhaps, the lost face that you
so long pursued looked up
from some daguerreotype—her steady eyes
deep in her own lake. Or when,
as dear, that idolized phantasm (almost
caught, in your gray-dawn dream) turned,
hollow-eyed, to look. Her stare so.
You understand that what was lost will not
be found. The plot winds ages back,
beyond statues that thaw and lovers' tag,
to its cold northern source. The moon
is thin: by sullen ones and twos
the fishers dot a frozen lake,
hunch hungry around a hole.

California

Zenas Leonard, mountain trapper wandering
westward, man with horse sense, hard-to-dazzle
connoisseur of croups and withers,
hocks and pasterns, even Zenas,
expert where men talked caballos,
rose up in his stirrups marveling:
there below him, great wild-horse herds
caracoled like butterflies
down the California valley.
Like a lecher who has tasted
only sweets that earth can offer, wakening
from a deeper nap than usual
arm in arm (through cosmic lapse) with
laughing henna-lidded houris
in Mahomet's paradise,
Zenas entered wild-horse heaven.

Riding past those mares and stallions
in the sunlit valley pastures, Zenas
hummed a tune for flashy pintos,
blue roan, milk white, all-black beauties,
smoky buckskins quick as foxes,
bays and sorrels trailing foals that
wobbled, lemon-tasseled chestnuts
rippling like the San Joaquin;
and, remembering, also celebrated
ponies that outran the Blackfeet's
when they had to, crowbait broomtails barely
worth their feed, that stolen army gelding—
Adams—who got stolen several more times,
hidden in a high-bluff pasture
appaloosas the Nez Perces
wouldn't trade for guns nor coffee;
and fell silent, recollecting
one longlost longlègged filly
(mountain scrambler with the supple
copper hide that he could hardly
keep his hands off, midnight mane)
lovelier than the Rose of Sharon
or than any Californian.

OPTIONAL NOTES

"Footnotes, like a cavalry escort to
a westering caravan, are a disturbing presence,
obtrusive, noisy, and dusty . . . . Our escort
should be just enough to get us through"
—Robert Ignatius Burns, S.J., *The Jesuits
and the Indian Wars of the Northwest*

"Calliope and Clio are not identical twins,
but they *are* sisters"
—Wallace Stegner, *The Sound of Mountain Water*

Though the debt varies, I owe something to all the writers whose books I mention (too briefly) in the following notes.

"Flute Song"

Osborne Russell's music-loving horses appear in *The Reminiscence of James Neall in Oregon and California 1845-50*, ed. Martin Schmitt and Keith Richard, Oregon Book Society, 1977.

"River Trader's Ledger"

Readers of Alexander Henry's journals may be reminded of his experiences, in Canada, among the Salteurs (*Journals of Alexander Henry and of David Thompson*, ed. Elliott Coues, 1897, Ross & Haines, 1965).

"Procession"

Major Osborne Cross reported in 1848 that "the cholera was not only in Saint Louis but had spread through every town on the Missouri River. . . . [It] raged with great violence on board several steamers, one of which after losing nearly thirty passengers, was entirely abandoned" (*The March of the Mounted Riflemen: First United States Military Expedition to Travel the Full Length of the Oregon Trail From Fort Leavenworth to Fort Vancouver, May to October, 1849, As Recorded in the Journals of Major Osborne Cross and George Gibbs and the Official Report of Colonel Loring*, ed. Raymond Settle, Arthur Clark, 1940).

"The Bone Hauler"

A capable man could skin fifty buffalo a day, according to buffalo hunter Dixon; he might receive $50 a month or 25¢ a hide (*Life of Billy Dixon, 1914*; Southwest Press, 1927). Stanley Vestal calculates: "It took four good men to skin a hundred buffalo in half a day" (*Queen of Cowtowns: Dodge City*, Harper, 1952). As for bones: "Freight trains . . . hauled bones to carbon works in St. Louis and other cities. There the newer bones were prepared for use in refining sugar, as the calcium phosphate neutralized the acid in cane juice. The old weather-beaten ones were ground into meal for sale as fertilizer. A few of the choice ones went into bone china" (Wayne Gard, *The Great Buffalo Hunt*, Knopf, 1965). Floyd Streeter estimates: "It required about one hundred carcasses to make one ton of bones; the price paid averaged eight dollars a ton" (*Prairie Trails & Cow Towns*, 1936; Devin Adair, 1963).

"Nuttall in Arkansa Territory"

Thomas Nuttall's *Journal of Travels into the Arkansa Territory, During the Year 1819, With Occasional Observations on the Manners of the Aborigines* was published in 1821. It is now vol. 13 in Reuben Thwaites' *Early Western Travels*. In 1818 Nuttall had published *The Genera of North American Plants*. A fine biography is Jeanette Graustein's *Thomas Nuttall, Naturalist*, Harvard Univ. Press, 1967.

"On a Blazed Tree by the Trail"

Emigrants' messages on trees, rocks, and boards "became a sort of combination bulletin board, newspaper and post office . . . . At the crossing of the Vermillion River in Kansas an army officer noted June 9, 1849: 'We found the trees and stumps on its banks carved all over with the names of hundreds of emigrants who had preceded us, the dates of their passing, the state of their health and spirits, together with an occasional message for their friends who were expected to follow'" (Grant Foreman, *Marcy & the Gold Seekers: The Journal of Capt. R.B. Marcy*, Univ. of Oklahoma Press, 1939).

"Lt. Montgomery Pike Harrison"

Lt. Harrison's death and posthumous journey in 1849 are reported in Foreman's *Marcy & the Gold Seekers* and in W. Eugene Hollon's *Beyond the Cross Timbers: The Travels of Randolph B. Marcy* (Univ. of Oklahoma Press, 1955). Marcy himself makes judicious references to these events in his *Prairie Traveler* (Harper, 1859) and *Thirty Years of Army Life on the Border* (1866; Lippincott, 1963).

"Grandfather"

In the first hundred pages of *Bad Medicine & Good: Tales of the Kiowas* (Univ. of Oklahoma Press, 1962), Wilbur Nye offers a useful summary of Kiowa history, describes the Tai-me medicine idols, and records in detail the Kiowas' sun dance ceremony. Two excerpts from Scott Momaday's *The Way to Rainy Mountain* (1969; Ballantine Books, 1973) are relevant: "The buffalo was the animal representative of the sun, the essential and sacrificial victim of the Sun Dance"; "The last Kiowa Sun Dance was held in 1887. . . . The buffalo was gone. In order to consummate the ancient sacrifice . . . a delegation of old men journeyed into Texas, there to beg and barter for an animal from the Goodnight herd."

"Mamanti"

Mamanti was a Kiowa medicine prophet. His powers are demonstrated in several of the stories Nye collected in *Bad Medicine & Good*.

"The Horse"

J. Frank Dobie discusses real and legendary white stallions in *The Mustangs* (Little Brown, 1952) and *Mustangs and Cow Horses* (Southern Methodist Univ. Press, 1940). Frank Roe surveys horse facts and legends in *The Indian and the Horse* (Univ. of Oklahoma Press, 1955).

"Against Big Bow"

In the stories Nye collected in *Bad Medicine & Good*, Big Bow is a loner and nonconformist, tough enough to deride even Mamanti and get away with it. To Thomas Battey, Big Bow is "the notorious Kiowa raider . . . who has, probably, killed and scalped more white people than any other living Kiowa" (*The Life and Adventures of a Quaker Among the Indians*, 1875; Univ. of Oklahoma Press, 1968).

"Kiowa Dutch"

In *Plains Indian Raiders* (Univ. of Oklahoma Press, 1968) Wilbur Nye provides the details in the poem's opening lines. The half-Cheyenne son of trader William Bent recalled: "Another captive my father bought was a German who was carried off by the Kiowas from the German colony in Texas when he was a small boy. He was known as Kiowa Dutch. He did not remain at the fort [Bent's trading post] long, but rejoined the Kiowas and became a regular wild Indian. He spoke nothing but Kiowa, and yet his features were typically German. He died among the Kiowas in 1906, about eighty-five years old" (George Hyde's *Life of George Bent*, ed. Savoie Lottinville, Univ. of Oklahoma Press, 1968).

"Thomas"

Thomas Battey was with the Caddoes and Kiowas from 1871 to 1874. The next year he published the fascinating book from which this poem derives, his *Life and Adventures of a Quaker Among the Indians*.

"Kicking Bird"

Battey described his friend Kicking Bird as "distinguished for eloquence, bravery, military capacity, good sound practical sense, and his friendship to the whites" (*Life and Adventures of a Quaker*). After their defeat by the U.S. Army in 1875, Kicking Bird had to select twenty-six Kiowas to be imprisoned at Fort Marion. To punish him, Mamanti "is supposed to have prayed Kicking Bird to death" (Nye, *Plains Indian Raiders*). An excerpt from Momaday's *The Way to Rainy Mountain* will account for the dog in the poem: "The principal warrior society of the Kiowas was the Ka-itsenko, 'Real Dogs' . . . . Tradition has it that the founder of the Ka-itsenko had a dream in which he saw a band of warriors . . . being led by a dog. The dog sang the song of the Ka-itsenko, then said to the dreamer: 'You are a dog; make a noise like a dog and sing a dog song.'"

"Lost Trapper"

Osborne Russell's *Journal* for the 1830s, edited by Aubrey Haines, was published in 1955 by the Oregon Historical Society.

"Variations on a Tale by Parkman"

In Parkman's version his scheme succeeds (chap. 14 of *The Oregon Trail, 1847*; Little Brown, 1925). The Enemy, Parkman's own name for his strange hypochondria, attacked him some years before his trip west and became worse in later years (*Letters of Francis Parkman*, vol. 1, ed. Wilbur Jacobs, Univ. of Oklahoma Press, 1960).

"Winter Quarters"

Sgt. Percival Lowe recalled conditions at his army post in Kansas about 1853: "The quarters were full of fleas, the old sod wall full of mice and snakes . . . . Compared to fleas, bedbugs are pets . . . . The two dozen cats that Lt. Heath brought from Fort Leavenworth two years before . . . could not digest mice enough to counteract the ravages of fleas" (*Five Years a Dragoon*, 1906; Univ. of Oklahoma Press, 1965).

"Buffalo"

Three buffalo were exhibited in 1868 in St. Louis and Chicago to promote the new stockyards at Abilene, Kansas. The first to describe their capture may have been Joseph G. McCoy in *Historic Sketches of the Cattle Trade of the West and Southwest*, 1874 (Arthur Clark, 1940).

"Dixie Lee"

Cowtowns followed the railroads west; women followed the cowtowns. Relevant memoirs include McCoy's *Historic Sketches of the Cattle Trade*, E.C. Abbott's *We Pointed Them North* (Farrar & Rinehart, 1939), and Stuart Henry's *Conquering Our Great American Plains* (Dutton, 1930).

"Ben Hodges, Colored"

Details of Hodges' life are in Robert Wright's *Dodge City: The Cowboy Capital and the Great Southwest* (1913; University Microfilms, Ann Arbor, 1959), Philip Durham and Everett Jones's *The Negro Cowboys* (Dodd Mead, 1965), Samuel Crumbine's *Frontier Doctor* (Dorrance, 1948), and William Katz's *The Black West* (Doubleday, 1973).

"The Legend"

"Careful men, if violent ones, real Westerners preferred to gun their enemies down with a shotgun from behind some convenient shelter; but in fantasy they walk toward each other forever, face to face, down sun-bright streets—ready for the showdown, which is to say, the last form of chivalric duel" (Leslie Fiedler, *The Return of the Vanishing American*, Stein & Day, 1968). Stuart Henry of Abilene, Kansas, bolsters the first half of Fiedler's assertion (*Conquering Our Great American Plains*).

The records and newspaper accounts collected by Nyle Miller and Joseph Snell in *Why the West Was Wild* (Kansas State Historical Society, 1963) show the disparity between Wyatt Earp's life and his legend. The legendary Earp is elaborately drawn in Stuart Lake's *Wyatt Earp: Frontier Marshal* (Houghton Mifflin, 1931), where he is "the greatest gunfighting marshal that the Old West knew." Lake bases some of his tales on the dubious testimony of Bat Masterson and much of the rest, he writes, on the recollections of old Wyatt Earp himself. The idealized Earp is reinforced by Vestal in

Queen of Cowtowns, 1952, by Richard O'Conner in *Bat Masterson* (Doubleday, 1957), and by Samuel Carter in *Cowboy Capital of the World* (Doubleday, 1973), among others. The debunked Earp appears in two books by Frank Waters, *The Colorado* (Rinehart, 1946) and *The Earp Brothers of Tombstone* (Clarkson Potter, 1960), in Harry Drago's *Wild, Woolly, & Wicked: The History of the Kansas Cowtowns* (Clarkson Potter, 1960), and in Peter Lyon's *The Wild, Wild West* (Funk & Wagnalls, 1969). In "The Wyatt Earp Syndrome" (*The American West*, May 1970), C.L. Sonnichsen discusses various fictional treatments of Earp.

"Prairie Dog Dave"

Prairie Dog Dave Morrow was variously known in the 1870s and '80s in Kansas as a buffalo hunter, Dodge City constable, deep drinker, and friend of Bat Masterson. Dave's genre here is the stretcher. His form is the ruptured sonnet. His plots are historically plausible; this pursuer-pursued yarn resembles one in Streeter's *Prairie Trails & Cow Towns*.

"A Story Dave Told"

In some stories of the old days, as in Dave's, Indian raiders have their stolen horses stolen (George Hyde, *Life of George Bent*; George Bird Grinnell, *The Fighting Cheyennes*, 1915, Univ. of Oklahoma Press, 1956; and Donald Berthrong, *The Southern Cheyennes*, Univ. of Oklahoma Press, 1963).

"A Toast to Prohibition"

Dave's story draws on anecdotes about Wild West pranks endured by lecturers—on phrenology, venereal ailments, Scripture, and temperance—who visited Dodge City in the 1870s and '80s (according to Miller and Snell, *Why the West Was Wild*; Wright, *Dodge City*; Vestal, *Queen of Cowtowns*; and Drago, *Wild, Wooly and Wicked*).

"False Teeth"

Dave elaborates a tale collected by John Stands in Timber and Margot Liberty (*Cheyenne Memories*, Yale Univ. Press, 1967). Trappers and others sometimes ingested gunpowder as seasoning or medicine.

"The Hermit"

Dave's plot resembles Wright's account in *Dodge City* of a buffalo that fell through the sod roof of a stagecoach station.

"Last Buffalo in Grant County"

The legend varied. As told by Col. Richard Dodge, the Cheyennes and Arapahoes believed the buffalo "are created within the bowels of the earth; that every year, when the young grass appears, herds of thousands pour out of two holes in the ground, and, under the direction of the Good God, depart on their long journeys to the countries of those tribes whom he desires especially to favor" (*Our Wild Indians: Thirty-Three Years' Personal Experience*, 1882; Books for Libraries Press, 1970). George Bird Grinnell records the Cheyenne legend of the very old woman living underground who gave both corn and buffalo to the Cheyennes (*The Cheyenne Indians*, vol. 2, Yale Univ. Press, 1923). Mari Sandoz refers to a Pawnee version of the legendary Buffalo Woman who, long ago, led animals and Indians to earth from a deep place underground (*The Buffalo Hunters*, Hastings House, 1954).

"Brick Bond"

Sometime during the 1870s Brick Bond may have killed 250 buffalo in one day, 1500 in one week, and 6000 in one season; the claims made for him vary. Later he ran a drugstore (which probably sold liquor) in Dodge City. Details are in Wright's *Dodge City*, Streeter's *Prairie Trails & Cow Towns*, and Vestal's *Queen of Cowtowns*. William Blackmore, an English sportsman, wrote: "In 1872, whilst on a scout for about a hundred miles south of Fort Dodge to the Indian Territory, we were never out of sight of buffalo. In the following autumn, on traveling over the same district, whilst the whole country was whitened with bleached and bleaching bones, we did not meet with buffalo until we were well into the Indian country, and then only in scanty bands. During this autumn, when riding some thirty to forty miles along the north bank of the Arkansas River to the east of Fort Dodge, there was a continuous line of putrescent carcases, so that the air was rendered pestilential and offensive to the last degree. The hunters had formed a line of camps along the banks of the river, and had shot down the buffalo, night and morning, as they came to drink" (Preface to Richard Dodge's *The Plains of the Great West*, 1876; Archer House, 1959).

"The Bugler"

The bugler at the Kiowa camp in 1866 may have been the bugler killed in the Indian attack at Adobe Walls in 1874. Though accounts differ, the man killed was more or less dark-skinned. Army Sgt. Herron, source for the scene in 1866, recalled also: "The bugler was a professional, but we never knew who he was as he never showed himself close enough to us to be recognizable." Herron's recollections are in Robert Wright's *Dodge City*, 1913. Hunters Billy Dixon and Bat Masterson were both at Adobe Walls in 1874. Dixon remembered the bugler as "a captive halfbreed Mexican" (*Life of Billy Dixon*, 1914). Masterson, in a letter written in 1913 about the battle, described the role of the "negro bugler," who may have been "a deserter from the [Negro] Tenth Cavalry" (in Miller and Snell's *Why the West Was Wild*). Quanah Parker, a Comanche leader in the battle at Adobe Walls, said in 1890: "One Comanche killed was a yellow nigger painted like Comanche. He had left nigger soldiers' company, everybody know that" (in Nye's *Bad Medicine & Good*).

"Captain Henry"

Guy V. Henry's words are quoted by Capt. Azor Nickerson in his manuscript "Major-General George Crook and the Indians" (in Martin Schmitt's *General George Crook: His Autobiography*, Univ. of Oklahoma Press, 1946 & 1960). Henry appears also in Capt. John Bourke's account of the battle at the Rosebud (*On the Border With Crook*, Scribners, 1892).

"Route 56"

At one time, Mari Sandoz writes in *Cheyenne Autumn* (1953; Avon Books, 1971), the Cheyennes "had a rich and mystical perception of . . . life as a continuous, all-encompassing eventual flow . . . . It was a stream . . . in which man . . . and all the other things were simultaneously in all the places they had ever been; and all things that had ever been in a place were always in the present there, in the being and occurring." Balanced accounts of Col. John Chivington's raid in 1864 include Stan Hoig's book *The Sand Creek Massacre* (Univ. of Oklahoma Press, 1961) and Grinnell's chronicle in *The Fighting Cheyennes*.

"Wolf Hunter's Squaw"

Robert Wright recalled trappers who "traded with the writer, and I seldom paid them less than six dollars apiece for their grey wolf skins." Wright remembered too the little swifts, prettier than foxes: "They were very susceptible to poison, and soon vanished from the face of the earth, as did the black croaking raven. I have seen the ground literally covered with dead ravens, for the space of an acre, around the carcasses of dead wolves that had been poisoned; having eaten of the flesh of the poisoned wolves, it affected the ravens the same as if they had eaten the poison direct" (*Dodge City*). General Nelson Miles recalled: "After taking the hide off the buffalo, the carcass would be poisoned in many cases, some yearling buffalo being generally selected, and next morning there might be found forty or fifty dead wolves lying scattered around, victims of the strychnine. In this way the large game was rapidly destroyed . . . . This might seem like cruelty and wasteful extravagance, but the buffalo, like the Indian, stood in the way of civilization and in the path of progress" (*Personal Recollections and Observations*, 1896; Da Capo Press, 1969).

"As for Scalp Shirts"
Additional lore will be found in Grinnell's *The Cheyenne Indians*, vol. 1, and in Hyde's *Life of George Bent*.

"When the Stars Fell"
A great meteor shower in November 1833 alarmed the Cheyennes, whose four sacred arrows had been captured by the Pawnees a few months earlier; since then, the Cheyennes had been expecting the worst (according to George Hyde, *Life of George Bent*, and David Lavender, *Bent's Fort*, Doubleday, 1954). Farther south, the Kiowas feared the meteors meant the end of the world. They had been expecting trouble since the year before, when their medicine idol, Tai-me, was stolen by a band of Osages (Momaday, *The Way to Rainy Mountain*).

"Flight"
Cholera struck the Plains tribes in 1849 and 1850 when emigrants on the Oregon Trail brought it up the Platte Valley. Emigrant William Buffington (himself Cherokee) recalled his arrival at the Platte in 1849: "Both sides of the river was a solid mass of wagons—men digging graves on each side of the river; men dying in their wagons, hallooing and crying and cramping with the cholera" (quoted by Foreman, *Marcy & the Gold Seekers*). George Bent wrote: "'Cramps' the Indians called it, and they died of it by hundreds. On the Platte whole camps could be seen deserted with the tepees full of dead bodies . . . . The Sioux and Cheyennes, who were nearest to the road, were the hardest hit, and from the Sioux the epidemic spread northward clear to the Blackfeet, while from the Cheyennes and Arapahos it struck down into the Kiowa and Comanche country . . . . Our [Cheyenne] tribe suffered very heavy loss; half of the tribe died, some old people say" (in Hyde's *Life of George Bent*). Wilbur Nye estimated that half the Kiowas and Comanches died from cholera (*Carbine and Lance*, Univ. of Oklahoma Press, 1943). Foreman's *Marcy & the Gold Seekers* has accounts of cholera in 1849 and 1850 on the Santa Fe Trail also.

"Mud Springs"
George Bent, a participant on the Indian side, is the chief source for details about the revenge-raid at Mud Springs Ranch in February 1865, three months after the Sand Creek disaster (in Hyde's *Life of George Bent*). As far as it goes, Grinnell's account in *The Fighting Cheyennes* supports George Bent's.

"The Trail"
The speaker shares some of the experiences of James Wilkins in *An Artist on the Overland Trail: The 1849 Diary and Sketches of James F. Wilkins*, ed. John Francis McDermott, Huntington Library, 1968. About a week west of Fort Laramie, Wilkins wrote: "Pass to day about 60 head of dead oxen on the road. This we presume is occasioned by poison [bad water] . . . besides a great deal of other property, wrecks of wagons, bacon [any pork] in piles, flour corn meal beans stoves ox chains, blacksmith tools crow bars, lead . . . and lastly gold-washers."

"Reading Carvalho's *Incidents of Travel*"
Solomon Carvalho was daguerreotypist for the fifth Fremont expedition, 1853-54. The poem develops a paragraph from his *Incidents of Travel* (1857; Arno Press, 1973). The last two lines go back to Han Shan, about the 8th century, who in turn was quoting a much older Chinese song (translated by Burton Watson in *Cold Mountain*, Columbia Univ. Press, 1970).

"According to Preuss"

Charles Preuss, one of the great secret-grumblers, was Fremont's cartographer on three expeditions, beginning in 1842. The first English translation of the lost diary Preuss wrote in German was published by the Univ. of Oklahoma Press in 1958, titled *Exploring with Fremont*, translated by Erwin and Elizabeth Gudde.

"Pages from De Smet"

Father De Smet's reports to his superiors were written in French and published in several languages, beginning in 1843. His 1843 and 1847 books are in Reuben Thwaites' *Early Western Travels*, vols. 27 and 29. A useful collection is Hiram Chittenden and Alfred Richardson's *Life, Letters, and Travels of Father Pierre-Jean De Smet, S.J., 1801-1873* (4 vols., Harper, 1905; Arno Press, 1969).

1 - This "special mark of heaven's favor" occurred on Christmas Eve 1841 at the new Flathead Mission. De Smet, who was there, reports the event in *Letters and Sketches*, Philadelphia, 1843 (Chittenden and Richardson, *Life, Letters . . .* , vol I). Father Nicolas Point, who was off hunting with other Flatheads, also reports it (*Wilderness Kingdom: Indian Life in the Rocky Mountains 1840-1847*, ed. Joseph Donnelly, S.J., Holt Rinehart Winston, 1967). 2 - This hunting took place in 1846, while De Smet was traveling with Blackfeet (Chittenden and Richardson, vol II). In chapters III and IV of *Wilderness Kingdom* Father Point describes the Indian buffalo hunts and shows them in his own paintings. 3 - De Smet's reports over the decades detail his baptizings; every soul counted. The Mandans, Grosventres, and Aricaras—whose village was on his Missouri River route to the Northwest—were "my old friends." This trip was made in 1864 (Chittenden and Richardson, vol. III).

"Drumhead Court"

Major Osborne Cross recorded desertions of teamsters and soldiers during the march to Oregon in 1849. A few men slipped away with mules and horses. Civilian George Gibbs, with Cross's expedition, described in his diary the mock court-martial of an emigrant found with stolen army horses. Both accounts are in *The March of the Mounted Riflemen*.

"Campfire Talk"

Tom's story comes from Green Majors' account of hundreds of buffalo mired in quicksand on the Upper Missouri (in Alexander Majors' *Seventy Years on the Frontier*, Ross & Haines, 1965). Col. Richard Dodge described a similar case, on the South Platte in 1867, where perhaps two thousand buffalo died (*The Plains of the Great West*).

"Will Drannan Tells It"

All four parts are based on recollections published by Rhodes & McClure, Chicago, in 1903: *Thirty-One Years on the Plains and in the Mountains ... . An Authentic Record of a Lifetime of Hunting, Trapping, Scouting, and Indian Fighting in the Far West, by Capt. William F. Drannan, Who Went on to the Plains when Fifteen Years Old*. Historian Leroy Hafen, who draws on Drannan's book in *The Mountain Men and the Fur Trade*, vol. 6, calls him "very unreliable in various particulars."

"The Revenge"

This Chisum ballad takes its plot from Frank Collinson, who said he had worked for years for John Chisum (*Life in the Saddle*, ed. Mary Clarke, Univ. of Oklahoma Press, 1963). Collinson wrote down his recollections originally for *Ranch Romances* (and perhaps romanced it a bit). Jack Schaefer praises Chisum for his generosity in *Heroes Without Glory*, Houghton Mifflin, 1965.

"Col. Fremont Broods"

The poem develops an incident in Fremont's third expedition, 1845. Fremont recorded it forty years later in his *Memoirs* (reprinted in vol. 2 of *The Expeditions of John Charles Fremont*, ed. Mary Spence and Donald Jackson, Univ. of Illinois Press, 1973).

"Old Bill"

The facts and conjectures come from four books: Alpheus Favour's *Old Bill Williams* (1936; Univ. of Oklahoma Press, 1962), William Brandon's *The Men and the Mountain* (1955; Greenwood Press, 1974), the diaries and letters collected by Leroy Hafen in *Fremont's Fourth Expedition* (Arthur Clark, 1960), and the Introduction by Donald Berthrong to W.T. Hamilton's *My Sixty Years on the Plains* (Univ. of Oklahoma Press, 1960).

"On the Upper Columbia"

The missionary poems which follow owe much to twelve volumes written or edited by Clifford Drury: *Henry Harmon Spalding* (Caxton, 1936), *Marcus Whitman, M.D.* (Caxton, 1937), *Elkanah and Mary Walker: Pioneers Among the Spokanes* (Caxton, 1940), *A Tepee in His Front Yard: A Biography of H.T. Cowley* (Binfords & Mort, 1949), *The Diaries and Letters of Henry H. Spalding and Asa Bowen Smith Relating to the Nez Perce Mission 1838-1842* (Arthur Clark, 1958), *First White Women Over the Rockies: Diaries, Letters, and Biographical Sketches of the Six Women of the Oregon Mission* (Arthur Clark, 3 vols., 1963-66), *Marcus and Narcissa Whitman and the Opening of Old Oregon* (Arthur Clark, 2 vols., 1973), *Nine Years with the Spokane Indians: The Diary 1838-1848 of Elkanah Walker* (Arthur Clark, 1976), and *Chief Lawyer of the Nez Perce Indians 1796-1876* (Arthur Clark, 1979).

The Walkers mention from time to time the Spokanes' starved dogs. The missionaries won the first battle, in 1839. But in 1845 Elkanah's journal included: "I have fitted up my saddles that the dogs ate up" (*Nine Years*). In 1843 Mary wrote: "The Big Star's dog killed our only cock and three hens" and in 1845 "Dog killed another hen, the third we have lost recently" (*First White Women*, II). Nicolas Point, S.J., found equally ravenous dogs with the Coeur d'Alenes and Flatheads: "The dogs spared nothing that smelled of animal. Leather receptacles, saddles, stirrups ... became prey to their rapacity" (*Wilderness Kingdom*).

"Mary Walker"

Mary's journal for June 1839 recorded the death of her new hens, on the trail between the Lapwai and Tshimakain missions. That day or the next, an Indian messenger overtook the Walkers with a message that Alice Whitman, the mission group's first child, had drowned. In part because of the troublesome hens, "Husband very much out of tune all day, scarce spoke pleasant" (*First White Women*, II).

"The Carpenters' Women"

Some of the tangled affairs of Campbell and Adams and their Indian wives can be traced in Mary Walker's journal for July-October 1843 and in Elkanah's for the same period. Mary occasionally mentioned her husband's aloofness during their nine years at Tshimakain: e.g., 1840, "What grieves me most is that the only being on earth with whom I can have much opportunity for intercourse manifests uniformly an unwillingness to engage me in social reading or conversation" (*First White Women*, II). They both complained, in their separate journals, of loneliness.

"A Page Not Sent"

Elkanah Walker from time to time deplored the Indians' apparent lack of interest in their souls and their adherence to their own medicine chants and dances. Over the years his sense of futility grew. Spokane Garry had been sent as a boy, by the Hudson's Bay Company, to the Anglican Mission School at Red River; but he was of only limited help to the missionaries, in part because the other Spokanes ridiculed his attempts to evangelize them (*Nine Years* and *First White Women*, II).

"The Independent"

Suggested by the last years of Asahel Munger, whose unraveling can be glimpsed in the letters and journals of the Walkers and Whitmans. Drury sums up what is known, in *Marcus and Narcissa Whitman*, I.

"Alice"

Narcissa Whitman's only child was born in March 1837 at Wailatpu Mission and drowned there in June 1839. Narcissa first received letters from home in July 1838, twenty-seven months after leaving home (Drury, *Marcus Whitman*, *M.D.* and *Marcus and Narcissa Whitman*).

Some letters crossed the Rocky Mountains in the 1830s with fur-company caravans, emigrants, and other travelers. The Hudson's Bay Company express across Canada, in the summer, also carried letters both ways. And letters, as well as boxes and barrels, came around Cape Horn, often via Honolulu. Into the 1840s, by any of these routes, letters might take a year to get from coast to coast (Drury, *Marcus and Narcissa Whitman*). In the 1850s, gold in California helped to create more options. Sailing ships continued going around Cape Horn. Packet boats in the Atlantic and Pacific connected with land crossings in Panama or Nicaragua. And overland mail-stage service between Missouri and California began—at first monthly, later weekly. In the 1860s came pony express and then the transcontinental railroads that soon replaced the ponies.

"Providence" & "Marcus Whitman"

The friend who went part of the way east with Whitman in the winter of 1842-43 was Asa Lovejoy. Drury sums up Lovejoy's accounts of their hard going in *Marcus and Narcissa Whitman*, II. Details in both poems come from Drury's volumes. The admiration is my own.

"Theophilos Degen"

This German doctor turns up briefly in at least two books, Drury's *Marcus and Narcissa Whitman*, II, and Erwin Thompson's *Shallow Grave at Waiilatpu* (Oregon Historical Society, rev. ed. 1973). The orphans are the Sager children, three of whom died with the Whitmans in 1847.

"Melting Time"

Spalding had his biggest success with the Nez Perces in the winter of 1838-39. At this period he sometimes employed ex-trappers Conner and Ebberts at the Lapwai Mission. Spalding thought by the end of 1838 that Conner would "prove a shining example of Almighty Grace," and in 1839 Conner did join the Mission Church (Ebberts seems to have disappeared). But early in 1841 Conner left for the Willamette Valley, "after doing me much injury" (*Diaries and Letters of Henry H. Spalding*).

"News from a Far Country"

Between labors, Spalding made time for long letter-reports. Chief sources are Drury's *Henry Harmon Spalding*, Drury's *Diaries and Letters of Henry H. Spalding*, and Eliza Spalding Warren's *Memoirs of the West* (Marsh Printing Co., 1916). Biblical phrases regularly season Spalding's correspondence.

"Temptation of John Townsend"

This misadventure is confessed in Townsend's *Narrative of a Journey Across the Rocky Mountains to the Columbia River . . . with a Scientific Appendix*, published in 1839, now vol. 21 in Thwaites' *Early Western Travels*.

The Presbyterian missionaries reached Fort Walla Walla in 1836. William Gray remembered they met young Dr. Townsend, "the naturalist": "He had been sent across the

Rocky Mountains, in company with Dr. Nuttall . . . by a society in Philadelphia, in 1834 . . . . He had remained in the country to complete his collection of specimens of plants and birds" (*History of Oregon 1792-1849*, 1870; Arno Press, 1973).

"California"

Leonard saw the California wild horses in 1833: "all very fat and . . . of all colors, from spotted or white, to jet blacks; and here, as in the land of civilization, they are the most beautiful and noble, as well as the most valuable of the whole brute creation" (*Adventures of Zenas Leonard, Fur Trader*, ed. John C. Ewers, Univ. of Oklahoma Press, 1959).